First World War
and Army of Occupation
War Diary
France, Belgium and Germany

GUARDS DIVISION
1 Guards Brigade
Headquarters
1 February 1917 - 28 February 1917

WO95/1213/5

The Naval & Military Press Ltd
www.nmarchive.com
Published in association with The National Archives

Published by

The Naval & Military Press Ltd

Unit 10 Ridgewood Industrial Park,

Uckfield, East Sussex,

TN22 5QE England

Tel: +44 (0) 1825 749494

www.naval-military-press.com

www.nmarchive.com

This diary has been reprinted in facsimile from the original. Any imperfections are inevitably reproduced and the quality may fall short of modern type and cartographic standards.

© **Crown Copyright**
Images reproduced by permission of The National Archives, London, England, 2015.

Contents

Document type	Place/Title	Date From	Date To
Heading	WO95/1213 Feb 1917		
Heading	HQ 1 Gds Bde. Vol 18.		
Heading	War Diary of Surgeon General W.W. Pike C.M.G., D.S.O. D.M.S. First Army From 1st January 1917 to 31st January 1917. With Appendices 1-36 (Volume 25.).		
War Diary	Billon Farm	01/02/1917	10/02/1917
War Diary	Billon Farm To Bois Douage	11/02/1917	13/02/1917
War Diary	Bois Douage	14/02/1917	26/02/1917
War Diary	Bois Douage To Billon Camps	27/02/1917	27/02/1917
War Diary	Billon Camps	28/02/1917	28/02/1917
Operation(al) Order(s)	Guards Division Order No. 108.	05/02/1917	05/02/1917
Miscellaneous	1st G.B. No. 1485.	06/02/1917	06/02/1917
Operation(al) Order(s)	Guards Division Order No. 107.	05/02/1917	05/02/1917
Miscellaneous	Movements Of Battalions During Relief. Appendix "A".		
Miscellaneous	Distribution Of Guards Brigades On Completion Of Relief. Appendix "B".		
Miscellaneous	Warning Order.	06/02/1917	06/02/1917
Miscellaneous	G.D. No. 2696/5/G.	08/02/1917	08/02/1917
Miscellaneous	G.D. No. 2696/5/G.	07/02/1917	07/02/1917
Miscellaneous			
Operation(al) Order(s)	1st Guards Brigade Order No. 100.	08/02/1917	08/02/1917
Miscellaneous	March Table To Be Attached To 1st Guards Brigade Order No. 100.		
Miscellaneous	1st Guards Bde. No. 1514.	08/02/1917	08/02/1917
Miscellaneous	1st Guards Brigade-Intelligence Report.	12/02/1917	12/02/1917
Miscellaneous	1st Guards Brigade-Intelligence Report.	13/02/1917	13/02/1917
Miscellaneous	1st Guards Brigade-Intelligence Report. 8.0 a.m. Feb. 13th To 8.30 a.m. Feb. 14th.	13/02/1917	13/02/1917
Miscellaneous			
Miscellaneous	1st Guards Brigade-Intelligence Report. 8 A.M. Feb: 14th To 8 A.M. Feb: 15th.	14/02/1917	14/02/1917
Miscellaneous	Intelligence Report-1st Guards Brigade. 8 A.M. Feb: 15th To 8 A.M. Feb: 16th.	15/02/1917	15/02/1917
Miscellaneous	Intelligence Report-1st Guards Brigade. 8 A.M. Feb: 16th-8 A.M. Feb: 17th.	16/02/1917	16/02/1917
Miscellaneous	1st Guards Brigade-Intelligence Report. 8 A.M. Feb: 17th To 8 A.M. Feb: 18th.	17/02/1917	17/02/1917
Miscellaneous	1st Guards Brigade-Intelligence Report. 8 A.M. Feb: 18th To 8 A.M. Feb: 19th.	18/02/1917	18/02/1917
Miscellaneous	1st Guards Brigade Intelligence Report. 8 A.M. Feb: 19th To 8 A.M. Feb: 20th.	19/02/1917	19/02/1917
Miscellaneous	1st Guards Brigade Intelligence Report. 8 A.M. Feb: 20th To 8 A.M. Feb: 21st.	20/02/1917	20/02/1917
Miscellaneous	1st Guards Brigade-Intelligence Report. 8 A.M. Feb: 21st To 8 A.M. Feb: 22nd.	21/02/1917	21/02/1917
Miscellaneous	1st Guards Brigade Intelligence Report. 8 A.M. Feb: 22nd To 8 A.M. Feb: 23rd.	22/02/1917	22/02/1917

Miscellaneous	1st Guards Brigade Intelligence Report. 8 A.M. Feb: 23rd To 8 A.M. Feb: 24th.	23/02/1917	23/02/1917
Operation(al) Order(s)	1st Guards Brigade Order No. 101.	23/02/1917	23/02/1917
Miscellaneous	March Table.		
Miscellaneous	G.D. No. 2696/5/G.	25/02/1917	25/02/1917
Miscellaneous			
Operation(al) Order(s)	Guards Division Order No. 109.	22/02/1917	22/02/1917
Miscellaneous	Movements Of Battalions & c. During Relief. Appendix "A".		
Miscellaneous	Distribution Of Guards Brigades On Completion Of Relief. Appendix "B".		
Miscellaneous	G.D. No. 2709/2/G.	22/02/1917	22/02/1917
Miscellaneous	1st Guards Brigade Intelligence Report. 8 A.M. Feb: 24th To 8 A.M. Feb: 25th.	24/02/1917	24/02/1917
Miscellaneous	1st Guards Brigade Order No. 102.	25/02/1917	25/02/1917
Operation(al) Order(s)	Guards Division Order No. 110.	23/02/1917	23/02/1917
Operation(al) Order(s)	Guards Division Order No. 111.	25/02/1917	25/02/1917
Miscellaneous	1st G.B. No. 1766.	26/02/1917	26/02/1917
Miscellaneous	Final Notes On The Line.		
Miscellaneous	Instructions No. 1 For Fregicourt Sector.	19/02/1917	19/02/1917
Miscellaneous	Instructions No. 1 For Fregicourt Sector.	08/02/1917	08/02/1917
Miscellaneous	Instructions No. 2 For Fregicourt Sector.	17/02/1917	17/02/1917
Miscellaneous	Instructions No. 3 For Fregicourt Sector.	09/02/1917	09/02/1917
Miscellaneous	1st Guards Bde. No. 1548.	10/02/1917	10/02/1917
Miscellaneous	Instructions No. 4 For Fregicourt Sector.	12/02/1917	12/02/1917
Miscellaneous	Instructions No. 5 For Fregicourt Sector.	14/02/1917	14/02/1917
Miscellaneous	Instructions No. 6 For Fregicourt Sector.	19/02/1917	19/02/1917
Miscellaneous	Amendment to 1st Guards Brigade Defence Scheme.	18/02/1917	18/02/1917
Miscellaneous	1st G.B. No. 1585/1.	17/02/1917	17/02/1917
Miscellaneous	1st Guards Brigade Defence Scheme.		
Miscellaneous	Appendix "B.1". Disposition Of Machine Guns.		
Miscellaneous	Appendix "B.2". Disposition Of Stocks Guns.		
Miscellaneous	Appendix "D"		
Miscellaneous	Appendix "E". Position Of Brigade Bomb And S.A.A. Stores.		
Miscellaneous	Appendix "A". Principles Of Defence		
Miscellaneous	Appendix "B". Gas Alert.		
Miscellaneous	1st Guards Bde. No. 1525.	09/02/1917	09/02/1917
Operation(al) Order(s)	1st Guards Brigade Defence Scheme.	09/02/1917	09/02/1917
Miscellaneous	Appendix "B.1". Disposition Of Machine Guns.		
Miscellaneous	Appendix "B.2". Disposition Of Stocks Guns.		
Miscellaneous	Appendix "D"		
Miscellaneous	G.D. No. 2691/1/G.	17/02/1917	17/02/1917
Miscellaneous	Appendix "D". Medical Arrangements For Attachment To Guards Division Defence Scheme.		
Miscellaneous	G.D. No. 2696/1/G.	14/02/1917	14/02/1917
Miscellaneous	Guards Division Defence Scheme.		
Miscellaneous	Appendix "A". Gas Attack.		
Miscellaneous	Appendix "B". S.O.S. And Counter Preparation.		
Miscellaneous	Counter Preparation And S.O.S.	11/02/1917	11/02/1917
Miscellaneous	Appendix 2. Counter Preparation And S.O.S. Appendix 2.		
Operation(al) Order(s)	Orders For Counter Preparation And S.O.S. Appendix "B".		
Miscellaneous	Appendix "C". Gas Alert.		
Map	Guards H.Q. 14.1.17.		

Map	M.G.D. 91/9.		
Map	M.G.D. 91/22.		
Operation(al) Order(s)	Amendment To Guards Division Order No. 112.	03/03/1917	03/03/1917
Operation(al) Order(s)	Guards Division Order No. 112.	26/02/1917	26/02/1917
Miscellaneous	Appendix "A". Movements Of Battalions Etc During Relief.		
Miscellaneous	Appendix "B". 2nd Guards Brigade.		
Diagram etc			
Operation(al) Order(s)	Amendment To Guards Division Order No. 112.	27/02/1917	27/02/1917
Miscellaneous	Appendix "A" Movements During Relief.		
Operation(al) Order(s)	1st Guards Brigade Order No. 103.	27/02/1917	27/02/1917

WO 95
12.13
Feb 1917

No 1 Ero Bd
Jr 18

On His Majesty's Service.

SECRET

War Diary
of
Surgeon-General W. W. Pike, C.M.G., D.S.O.
D.M.S. First Army.
From 1st January 1917 to 31st January. 1917.
With Appendices 1–36.
(Volume 25).

Army Form C. 2118.

February 1917
H.Q. 1st Bn John Bole

WAR DIARY
or
INTELLIGENCE SUMMARY

(Erase heading not required.)

Instructions regarding War Diaries and Intelligence Summaries are contained in F.S. Regs., Part II. and the Staff Manual respectively. Title Pages will be prepared in manuscript.

Place	Date	Hour	Summary of Events and Information	Remarks and references to Appendices
BILLON FARM.	Feb 1st		Training of Lewis Gunners & Bombers carried out as usual.	JBB
	Feb 2nd		1st Bn Coldm Gds moved to PRIEZ FARM & relieved the 3rd Coldstream Gds as reserve to Camp 107. at BILLON.	
	Feb 3.		3rd Coldstream carried out coy practise attacks over some old trenches near BILLON Wood. Casualties at work Pte Capt. J. ORR & 2.O.R wounded.	
	Feb 4th		Church services as usual in the morning.	
	Feb 5th		3rd Bn Grenadier Gds carried out a practise assault from trenches. Brigadier & Bde Major witnessed a practise attack carried out by a French Training Bn. - The attack was carried out with live ammunition & bombs - The infantry put down an effective barrage with bombs & rifle grenades. The effect of the bombs offered very local by the barrage was felt to be thick enough to stop any enemy getting through it. The infantry advanced firing Lewis guns from the hip -	

WAR DIARY or INTELLIGENCE SUMMARY

Army Form C. 2118.

Place	Date	Hour	Summary of Events and Information	Remarks and references to Appendices
BILLON FARM	Feb 5.		Bde Jnr Orders No 107 & 108 received.	app 305 " 306.
	Feb 6.		1st Bn Rifle Bde No 1485 issued. 3rd Coldstream Bn carried out practice assault from trenches. 2nd Bn Gren Gds bathing.	" 307.
	Feb 7.		The northern edge of BILLON wood was shelled by an 11 inch gun — arrived at the PLATEAU Railhead.	
	Feb 8.	2 pm	A.D.V.S. inspected Transport horses of the Brigade. 1st Gds Bde Orders No 100 issued.	309
	Feb 9.		3rd Coldstream Bn moved to MAUREPAS. Bde in Support T.M.By instructions. 3rd Coldstream Bn relieved 2nd Scots Gds in left subsector of FRÉGICOURT sector.	310
	Feb 10.		3rd Gren Gds moved to MAUREPAS. No 2.Coy & T.M. BY moved into the line.	311.

Army Form C. 2118.

WAR DIARY
or
INTELLIGENCE SUMMARY

(Erase heading not required.)

Place	Date	Hour	Summary of Events and Information	Remarks and references to Appendices
BILLON FARM to BOIS DONAGE 	Feb.12.	3 p.m.	Bde. H.Q. closed at BILLON camp & opened at BOIS DONAGE. 2nd Gren. Bn. relieved 1st Gren. Bn. in right subsector. 2nd Coldstream Bn. moved from PRIEZ to MAUREPAS. Casualties to 12 noon:— 3rd Coldstream Bn. O.R. wounded 1. Missing 1. 3rd Coldstream Bn. O.R. " 1.	
	Feb.12.		A very quiet night & enemy artillery inactive in Bde sector. Casualties nil.	Intelligence App. 3/12.
	Feb.13.		Another quiet night. Casualties 3rd Colds. Bn. O.R. wounded 1.	Intelligence " 3/13
		3 to 4 p.m.	Our artillery carried out a bombardment of enemy trenches in about U.21. central. 1st Bn. Bde. M.G. Coy brought rapid rifle & M.G. fire to bear on these trenches. Towards the end of the bombardment enemy retaliated on our trenches in the left flank of the Bde.	
		3.30 p.m.	Enemy aeroplane brought down by A.A. fire near Bn. Bde. H.Q. at U.19.d.3.5½.	

Army Form C. 2118.

WAR DIARY
or
INTELLIGENCE SUMMARY
(Erase heading not required.)

Instructions regarding War Diaries and Intelligence Summaries are contained in F.S. Regs., Part II. and the Staff Manual respectively. Title Pages will be prepared in manuscript.

Place	Date	Hour	Summary of Events and Information	Remarks and references to Appendices
Bois Douai E.	Feb. 14th		Casualties 3rd Coldstream Gds wounded O.R. 3.	Intelligence appx. 314.
"	Feb. 15th		A very quiet day. Enemy active on 50th Bde sector on our left — enemy aeroplanes also very active & flying low during the afternoon — 3rd Coldstream Gds relieved 3rd Coldstream Gds in left subsector.	
			During the afternoon the artillery on both sides was very active — but no damage was done in the Bde area. 1st Irish Gds to relieved 2nd Gren Gds. T.M.By (3 C.G.) o.R. wounded 1. Casualties 1st Irish Bde T.M.By (3 C.G.) o.R. wounded 1.	Intelligence appx. 315.
"	Feb. 16th		Enemy artillery again rather more active than usual. In the evening a detachment from 357 Regt came into the lines of 2nd Bn Coldm Gds — subsequently gave some very useful information.	
			Casualties 2nd Gren Bn. o.R. wounded 2. 2nd Coldm Gds " " 1. 1st Coldm Gds o.R. " 1. Bde T.M. Coy o.R. " 1.	Intelligence appx. 316.

WAR DIARY
or
INTELLIGENCE SUMMARY

Army Form C. 2118.

Place	Date	Hour	Summary of Events and Information	Remarks and references to Appendices
BOIS DOUAGE 	Feb.17th		An extremely quiet day owing to thick mist - A thaw had now really set in but the ground underneath was still too hard to permit of digging - Casualties 1st Irish Gds. O.R. wounded 1. 1st Bn Bob 3.f. Gy. O.R. " 2.	Intelligence 317
	Feb.18th		Again + misty + quiet. Found too hard for digging - Casualties 2nd Coldstream Gds. O.R. wounded 1. 1st Irish Gds. O.R. wounded 3. 3rd Cold Gds relieved 2nd Cold Gds in left sub-sector.	Intelligence 318
	Feb.19th		Another misty day but quiet - Ground still too hard underneath for digging. Casualties B.M.G. SEELEY wounded. 2nd Gren Gds relieved 1st Irish Gds in right sub sector -	Intelligence 319
	Feb.20th		A wet day. About midday enemy shelled reserve line of right sub with 5.9's Casualties 2nd Bn Gren Gds O.R. killed 1.	Intelligence 320

WAR DIARY or INTELLIGENCE SUMMARY

Army Form C. 2118.

Place	Date	Hour	Summary of Events and Information	Remarks and references to Appendices
BOIS DULAGE 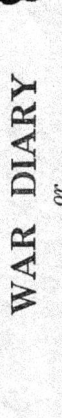	Feb 21st		Very misty all the morning & very quiet until spur when enemy put down a very heavy barrage along the left Bn. front & half the right Bn. front. Two unlucky shells direct hits on No 10 support post caused 8 casualties in that post alone but otherwise little damage was done. The shelling died down at 8pm. The cause of this sudden outburst is not known but it is thought that the enemy may have suspected a relief. Casualties to 12 noon Lieut Q.S. GREENE 3rd Bn Coldstream Gds wounded	APP 322 Intelligence off.
	Feb 22		Again very misty during the morning — a very quiet day Casualties 2nd Bn Gds wounded Lieut A. Mc.W. LAWSON-JOHNSON M.C. Lieut R. TERRELL	Intelligence off. 323
			3rd Coldstream Gds wounded at duty Lt R.T. FOSTER O.R. killed 2 wounded 13 (1 at duty) Bde M.G. Cy. O.R. wounded 1. 2nd Coldm Gds relieved 3rd Coldstream Gds in right sector. Sp. Div Order 20 received	App 324

Army Form C. 2118.

WAR DIARY
or
INTELLIGENCE SUMMARY
(Erase heading not required.)

Instructions regarding War Diaries and Intelligence Summaries are contained in F. S. Regs., Part II. and the Staff Manual respectively. Title Pages will be prepared in manuscript.

Place	Date	Hour	Summary of Events and Information	Remarks and references to Appendices
BOIS DOUAGE	Feb 23		Very misty in morning but lifted sufficiently in afternoon to allow a bombardment of an enemy strong point in Left Bn area. About 8 pm enemy put down heavy barrage along right Bn front & this worked its way up to Left Bn front & then passed away to the North. No damage was done. Casualties Nil.	
		8pm	1st Bn Bde Order No 101 issued. 1st Bn Irish Fus relieved 2nd Bn Irish Fus in right sector.	Appx 325
	Feb 24		Our artillery carried out wire cutting on Left Bn front. This occurred to attract little retaliation. 1st Irish Fus O.R. Killed 3. wounded 8. Casualties Nil.	Appx 326 Appx 327
	Feb 25		Quiet day - snowing again - stated shelling Left Bn area about 6 pm. Casualties Nil. 1st Fus Bde Order No 102 issued.	Intelligence 328 329

2449 Wt. W14957/M90 750,000 1/16 J.B.C. & A. Forms/C.2118/12.

Place	Date	Hour	Summary of Events and Information	Remarks and references to Appendices
R903 DOURGE	Feb 28th		Some nightly patrol work was done during night of 25/28th Feb. an information being received that enemy intended carrying out a retirement in front of our sector. Five patrols went out & succeeded in all cases in reaching the enemy wire. All patrols were seen & fired on but the fact was established that the enemy was on the alert & holding his line strongly.	
			Casualties 2nd Coldm. Gds. Lt. D.S. BROWN. wounded	
			O.R. wounded 4.	
			2nd Coldstream Gds. relieved by 2nd Irish Gds. Enemy put down heavy barrage along PERONNE road at 6pm just too early to catch relief. This barrage affects almost a nightly occurrence	
			Gds Div Order No 112 received	App 333
			Defence Scheme's final notes on the true attached herewith	App 334

Army Form C. 2118.

WAR DIARY
or
INTELLIGENCE SUMMARY

(Erase heading not required.)

Instructions regarding War Diaries and Intelligence Summaries are contained in F. S. Regs., Part II. and the Staff Manual respectively. Title Pages will be prepared in manuscript.

Place	Date	Hour	Summary of Events and Information	Remarks and references to Appendices
BOIS DONAGE to BILLON Camp	Feb 18th 29.		Again good patrols were carried out during night & enemy found alert. Our artillery were ordered to cut wire & force Right Bn. front with view to a possible raid but this raid was not to be carried out for some days. 17th Irish Regt. relieved by 3rd Bn. Grenadier Gds. at 7pm. Bde Order No. 103 issued.	AEP 335.
BILLON Camp	Feb 20th		At 10a Irish Gds moved to BILLON Camp 16. Units employed on fatigues & cleaning up.	

[signature]
Lt Col.
Commanding 1st Irish Gds.

SECRET.   306   Copy No. 5

GUARDS DIVISION ORDER NO. 108.

1.   The 17th Division, on the morning of 8th February at a zero hour to be notified later, are to carry out an attack on hostile trenches from U.15.c.05.70 to U.14.b.85.20.

2.   Guards Divisional Artillery will cooperate with this attack as follows. (Details of allotment of ammunition and rates of fire have been communicated to G.O.C. R.A.)

(a)   A field artillery barrage to commence at zero on enemy's front line between U.21.a.5.5 and U.26.a.6.6.

X V Corps are extending this barrage South of C.2.a.8.10. Barrage to cease at zero + 15 minutes, with the exception of battery firing on flank nearest to 17th Divn.

(b)   A smoke barrage from 4.5" howitzers to commence at zero on the line U.21.a.0.4 - U.15.d.5.0. This barrage to continue as long as the ammunition allotted will permit, but must be at its thickest from zero to zero + 15 minutes.

(c)   A smoke barrage from 4.5" howitzers to commence at zero on the line U.26.a.7.6 - U.26.b.7.6 (SCHUBERT TRENCH), and to continue as long as ammunition allotted will permit.

(d)   Likely assembly areas in U.21.b,c and d will be shelled at intervals from zero to zero + 48 hours.

3.   3rd Guards Brigade will arrange machine gun barrages as under:-

(a)   In cooperation with the right of the attack.

3rd Guards Brigade have been informed of detailed requirements of 17th Division in this respect by G.O.C. 52nd Inf. Bde.

(b)   Onto the valley U.21.c.5.10 - 10.3.

Barrage on this area will be maintained at intervals throughout the night of 8th/9th February, and will also be opened at any time after zero if enemy show activity or signs of massing for counter attack.

4. When the French carried out an attack last November similar to that to be undertaken by the 17th Division, the enemy counter attacked from the direction of ST. PIERRE VAAST WOOD.

3rd Guards Brigade will ensure that from zero onwards a careful watch is kept on ST. PIERRE VAAST WOOD, so that any massing of enemy's infantry on our front may be detected and dealt with, by means of artillery, rifle and machine gun fire.

5. Watches will be synchronised from Divisional Headquarters at 7.30 p.m. on February 7th.

A C K N O W L E D G E.

C P Heyworth
Lieut-Colonel,
General Staff. Guards Divn.

5th February 1917.

Issued to Signals at 7.30 p.m.

Copy No.				
1	General Staff.		8	Pioneer Battalion.
2	"Q".		9	Signals.
3	G.D.A.		10	A.D.M.S.
4	C.R.E.		11	XIV Corps.
5	1st Guards Brigade.		12	8th Division.
6	2nd Guards Brigade.		13	17th Division.
7	3rd Guards Brigade.		14	War Diary.

****

SECRET.   307   1st G.B. No. 1485

```
2nd Bn. Grenadier Guards.        1st Guards T.M. Battery.
2nd Bn. Coldstream Guards.       1st Gds. Bde. Supply Officer.
3rd Bn. Coldstream Guards.       1st Gds. Bde. Transport Officer.
1st Bn. Irish Guards.            2nd Guards Brigade.
Bde., Machine Gun Company.       3rd Guards Brigade.
```

1. The following is a table of moves to be carried out by Units of the Brigade between Feb: 9th and Feb: 12th.

2. Detailed orders for relief will be issued later.

3.

Date.	Unit.	From.	To.
Feb: 9th.	2/Cold.Gds.	Camp 107	MAUREPAS.
"	1st Gds.Bde. M.G.Coy & T.M.Bty.	Camp 16	MAUREPAS.
Feb:10th	2/Gren.Gds.	Camp 107	MAUREPAS.
"	2/Cold.Gds.	MAUREPAS.	Left Sub-sector.
"	1st Gds.Bde. M.G.Coy & T.M.Bty.	MAUREPAS.	Line.
Feb:11th.	2/Gren.Gds.	MAUREPAS.	Right Sub-sector.
"	3/Cold.Gds.	PRIEZ Farm.	MAUREPAS.
Feb:12th.	1/Irish Gds.	Camp 16.	MAUREPAS.

ACKNOWLEDGE.

                                                Captain,
8th February 1917.   Brigade Major, 1st Guards Brigade.

SECRET.   Copy No ...5...

GUARDS DIVISION ORDER NO. 107.

1. (a) 1st Guards Brigade will relieve 3rd Guards Brigade in the line on the nights 10th/11th and 11th/12th February.

   Details of reliefs to be arranged between Brigades concerned.

   (b) On relief, 3rd Guards Brigade will move back into Corps Reserve area (VILLE - TREUX - MERICOURT).

   (c) 2nd Guards Brigade will move into the BILLON area (2nd Bn. Irish Guards at PRIEZ FARM) and will become Divisional reserve.

   (d) 75th Field Coy. will relieve 55th Field Coy. in the line, the latter moving on relief to BRONFAY FARM.

   76th Field Coy. will move from BRONFAY to MAUREPAS.

   All movements to be carried out in accordance with Appendix 'A' attached.

   Details of routes and times of starting will be issued later.

2. 3rd Guards Brigade will take over all Corps Working Parties now found by 2nd Guards Brigade. Detailed arrangements will be made between Guards Brigades concerned, and will be such as to ensure that there is no hiatus in the work.

3. Disposition of Guards Brigades etc., on completion of relief is shewn in Appendix 'B' attached.

4. During the process of relief, G.Os.C. Guards Brigades will have under their tactical command all battalions in their respective Brigade areas.

ACKNOWLEDGE.

                                                    Lieut. Colonel,
5th Feb. 1917.   General Staff, Guards Division.

Issued to Signals at 6.30 p.m.

Copy No.1 General Staff.	10. A.D.M.S.	19 Camp Cmdt: MAUREPAS.
2 "Q"	11 A.D.V.S.	20 Camp Cmdt: BILLON.
3 C.D.A.	12 A.P.M.	21 Camp Cmdt: BRONFAY.
4 C.R.E.	13 Train.	22 Town Major: VILLE.
5 1st Guards Bde.	14 S.S.C.	23 -do- MERICOURT.
6 2nd Guards Bde.	15 D.A.D.C.S.	24 -do- TREUX.
7 3rd Guards Bde.	16 8th Division.	25 War Diary.
8 Pioneer Battn.	17 17th Division.	
9 Divnl. Signals.	18 XIV Corps.	

Appendix 'A'.

MOVEMENTS of BATTALIONS during RELIEF.

Date.	Unit.	From.	To.	Remarks.
Feb. 9.	4/Grenadier Guards.	MAUREPAS.	VILLE.	Rail from PLATEAU.
	1/Coldstream Guards.	VILLE.	BILLON.	
	3/Coldstream Guards.	BILLON.	MAUREPAS.	
	1st Gds.Bde.M.G.Coy. & T.M.Bty.	BILLON.	MAUREPAS.	
	2nd Gds.Bde.M.G.Coy & T.M.Bty.	TREUX.	BILLON.	
Feb.10.	1/Welsh Guards.	MAUREPAS.	MERICOURT.	Rail from PLATEAU.
	2/Grenadier Guards.	BILLON.	MAUREPAS.	
	3/Grenadier Guards.	MERICOURT.	BILLON.	
	2/Scots Guards.	LINE.	MAUREPAS.	
	2/Coldstream Guards.	MAUREPAS.	LINE (Left Sector).	
	3rd Gds.Bde.M.G.Coy & T.M.Bty.	LINE.	MAUREPAS.	
	1st Gds.Bde.M.G.Coy. & T.M.Bty.	MAUREPAS.	LINE.	
	55th Field Coy.R.E.	CORLES.	VRONFAY.	
	75th Field Coy.R.E.	MAUREPAS.	CORLES.	
	76th Field Coy.R.E.	MONFAY.	MAULTPAS.	

Page. 2.

Date.	Unit.	From.	To.	Reports.
Feb.11.	2/Coldstream Guards.	PRIEZ FARM.	MAUREPAS.	
	2/Irish Guards.	VILLE.	PRIEZ FARM.	Rail to PLATEAU (or bus to MAUREPAS).
	1/Grenadier Guards.	LINE.	MAUREPAS.	
	2/Grenadier Guards.	MAUREPAS.	LINE (Right Sector).	
	2/Scots Guards.	MAUREPAS.	VILLE.	Rail from PLATEAU.
Feb.12.	1/S.GRENADIER Guards.	MAUREPAS.	MERICOURT.	Rail from PLATEAU.
	1/Scots Guards.	MERICOURT.	BILLON.	
	1/Irish Guards.	BILLON.	MAUREPAS.	
	3rd Gds.-de.M.G.Coy & T.M.Bty.	MAUREPAS.	TREUX.	To move on 11th 249/6/c

Appendix 'B'.

DISTRIBUTION of GUARDS BRIGADES on COMPLETION of RELIEF.

Brigade in the Line.	Divisional Reserve.	Corps Reserve.
1st Guards Brigade.	**2nd Guards Brigade.**	**3rd Guards Brigade.**
Brigade Hd.Qrs. = BOIS DOUAGE at B.4.c.5.2.	Brigade Hd. Qrs. = BILLON.	Brigade Hd. Qrs. = VILLE.
3/Coldstream Guards = LINE (Left).	1/Coldstream Guards = BILLON.	4/Grenadier Guards = VILLE.
2/Grenadier Guards = LINE (Right).	1/Scots Guards = BILLON.	2/Scots Guards = VILLE.
1st Gds.BDE M.G.Coy & T.M.Baty. = LINE.	3/Grenadier Guards = BILLON.	1/Welsh Guards = MERICOURT.
1/Irish Guards = MAUREPAS.	2/Irish Guards = PRIEZ FARM.	1/Grenadier Guards = MERICOURT.
2/Coldstream Guards = MAUREPAS.	2nd Gds.Bde.M.G.Coy & T.M.Baty. = BILLON.	3rd Gds.Bde.M.G.Coy & T.M.Baty. = TREUX.
75th Field Coy.R.E. = COMBLES.	55th Field Coy.R.E. = BROEFAY.	

SECRET.   2.G.B.No.541/G.

3rd. Bn. Grenadier Guards.   Bde. Supply Officer.
1st. Bn. Coldstream Guards.   1st. Guards Brigade.
1st. Bn. Scots Guards.   3rd. Guards Brigade.
2nd. Bn. Irish Guards.   Guards Division.
Bde. M. G. Company.   Staff Captain.
=============================   =========================

WARNING ORDER
-:*:---------------:*:-

1. 2nd. Guards Brigade will relieve 1st. Guards Brigade in
   Divisional Reserve at BILLON FARM between February 9th. and
   12th.

2. Units will move as follows:-

Date.	Unit.	From.	To.
Feb. 9th.	1/C.G.	VILLE.	BILLON.
	M. G. COY.	TREUX.	BILLON.
" 10th.	3/G.G.	MERICOURT.	BILLON.
" 11th.	Bde. Hqrs.	VILLE.	BILLON.
	2/I.G.	VILLE.	PRIEZ FARM.
" 12th.	1/S.G.	MERICOURT.	BILLON.

3. 2 Coys of 1st. Bn. Scots Guards at present finding Decauville
   fatigue at BRIQUETERIE will be relieved on February 9th. and
   will rejoin Battalion at MERICOURT.

4. Units will move to PRIEZ FARM in the following order :-

   February 11th.   -   2nd. Bn. Irish Guards.
   "   15th.   -   3rd. Bn. Grenadier Guards.
   "   19th.   -   1st. Bn. Coldstream Guards.
   "   23rd.   -   1st. Bn. Scots Guards.

5. Units will forward to Bde. Hqrs. by February 8th. a report
   in duplicate showing location of all parade grounds, bombing
   grounds, bayonet practice grounds and rifle ranges in use at
   their respective billets.

   These will be forwarded to 3rd. Guards Brigade for relieving
   Battalions.

   ACKNOWLEDGE.
   =======================

   6/2/17.
   =======   Captain.
                                                 Brigade Major.

G.D.No. 2696/5/G

C.R.E.
1st Guards Brigade.
2nd Guards Brigade.
3rd Guards Brigade.
Town Major, VILLE,
Camp Comdt, MAUREPAS.
"Q".

Reference G.D.No. 2696/5/G of the 7th and March Table attached, on February 11th 2nd Bn. Coldstream Guards will clear PRIEZ FARM at noon.

2nd Bn. Irish Guards will march from VILLE to PRIEZ, clearing VILLE by 8 a.m.   Route - MEAULTE, MARICOURT, HARDECOURT.

E. Seymour.

8th Feb. 1917.

Captain G.S.,
Guards Division.

SECRET

G.D. No.2696/5/G.

"Q".	S.S.O.
G.D.A.	D.A.D.O.S.
C.R.E.	8th Division.
1st Guards Brigade.	17th Division.
2nd Guards Brigade.	XIV Corps.
3rd Guards Brigade.	Camp Comdt. MAUREPAS.
Pioneer Battalion.	Camp Comdt. BILLON.
Divnl. Signals.	Camp Comdt. BRONFAY.
A.D.M.S.	Town Major VILLE.
A.D.V.S.	Town Major. MERICOURT.
A.P.M.	Town Major. TREUX.
Divnl. Train.	

March Table giving routes and times of starting for movements ordered in Guards Division Order No. 107 is attached.

ACKNOWLEDGE.

7th February 1917.

E. Seymour
Captain,
General Staff. Guards Divn.

DATE	UNIT	FROM		ROUTE	REMARKS
Feb. 9th.	4th Gren: Guards	MAUREPAS	VILLE	March to PLATEAU; thence by rail. Transport by road via MARICOURT - FRICOURT - MEAULTE.	To clear Camp by 9.30 a.m. To clear transport lines by 7.30 a.m.
	1st Cold: Guards	VILLE	BILLON	MORLANCOURT - K.21.b.8.8 - BRAY	To be clear of VILLE by 9 a.m. 10.30am
	3rd Cold: Guards	BILLON	MAUREPAS	MARICOURT - HARDECOURT	To clear BILLON Camp by 8.30 a.m.
	1st Gds.Bde.M.G. Co. & T.M.Batt.	BILLON	MAUREPAS	MARICOURT - HARDECOURT	To clear BILLON Camp by 9 a.m.
	2nd Gds.Bde.M.G. Co. & T.M.Batt.	TREUX	BILLON	CARCAILLOT Cross roads - L.15.b.	To pass CARCAILLOT 10 a.m.
Feb.10th.	1st Welsh Guards	MAUREPAS	MERICOURT	March to PLATEAU; thence by rail. Transport by road via MARICOURT - FRICOURT - MEAULTE.	Bn. to clear Camp by 9.30 a.m. Transport to clear lines by 7.30 a.m.
	2nd Gren: Guards	BILLON	MAUREPAS	MARICOURT - HARDECOURT	To clear BILLON Camp by 8.30 a.m.
	3rd Gren: Guards	MERICOURT	BILLON	J.22.b.7.9 - BRAY	To be clear of MERICOURT by 10 a.m.
	55th Field Co.R.E.	COMBLES	BRONFAY	HARDECOURT - MARICOURT	
	75th Field Co.R.E.	MAUREPAS	COMBLES		Not to move before noon.
	76th Field Co.R.E.	BRONFAY	MAUREPAS	MARICOURT - BRONFAY	

DATE.	UNIT.	FROM.	TO.	ROUTE.	REMARKS.
Feb. 11th.	2nd Cold: Guards	PRIEZ FARM	MAUREPAS		
	2nd Irish Guards	VILLE	PRIEZ FARM		
	2nd Scots Guards	MAUREPAS	VILLE	March to PLATEAU, thence by rail Transport by road via MARICOURT - FRICOURT - MEAULTE.	To clear Camp by 9.30 a.m. Transport to clear lines by 7.30 a.m.
	H.Q. 2nd Guards Bde.	VILLE	BILLON	} Under Brigade arrangements	
	H.Q. 1st Guards Bde.	BILLON	BOIS DOUAGE		
Feb. 12th.	1st Grens Guards	MAUREPAS	MARICOURT	March to PLATEAU, thence by rail Transport by road via MARICOURT - FRICOURT - MEAULTE.	Bn. to clear Camp by 9.30 a.m. Transport to clear lines by 7.30 a.m.
				J.22.b.7.9 - BRAY	To be clear of MARICOURT by 10 a.m.
	1st Scots Guards	MARICOURT	BILLON		
	1st Irish Guards	BILLON	MAUREPAS	MARICOURT - LARDEJOURT	To clear BILLON by 8.30 a.m.
	3rd Gds.Bde.M.G. Co.& T.M.Batt.	MAUREPAS	TREUX	Personnel march to PLATEAU in rear of 1st Gren:Gds; thence by rail. Transport by road via MARICOURT - FRICOURT.	Transport to clear lines by 7.30 a.m.

1. Transport will march with Battalions, except where otherwise ordered.

2. All movements of troops East of and including MEAULTE will be by Companies in file at 200 yards interval between Companies and 500 yards between Battalions.

3. Troops moving on BRAY - MARICOURT road will do so at intervals of 500 yards between Companies.

4. Trains will leave PLATEAU at 11.30 a.m. on 9th, 10th, 11th, and 12th Feby.

SECRET.   309   Copy No. 17

1st Guards Brigade Order No.100.

Ref. Map - ALBERT Combined
Sheet 1/40,000.   February 8th, 1917.

1. The 1st Guards Brigade will relieve the 3rd Guards Brigade in the line from U 26 c 9.4 to U 24 b 4.3 in accordance with attached March Table, further details of relief will be arranged direct between Units concerned.

2. Details of relief of Machine Gun Coy's and Trench Mortar Bty's will be arranged direct between O.C's concerned.

3. Until 3 P.M. on Feb: 11th Units of 1st Guards Brigade in forward area will come under Orders of G.O.C., 3rd Guards Brigade.

   Similarly Units of 2nd Guards Brigade in the BILLON Farm area will come under Orders of G.O.C., 1st Guards Brigade.

4. (a) Billeting parties of Units moving into the Camps at MAUREPAS will report to the Town Majors Office in the MAUREPAS RAVINE.

   (b) Battalions moving into the line will send forward an advanced party of not less than 1 N.C.O. per Company and per Battn., H.Q., to report at Battn., H.Q., in the line on the evening before their Battn's move into the line.

5. (a) 1st Line Transport will move in rear of Units, an interval of 100 yards being left between every 4 vehicles.

   (b) Transport Lines will be taken over as follows :-

   Feb: 9th 3rd Bn.Cold.Gds. from 4th Bn.Gren.Gds. at B 13 a 4.6.
   "   10th 2nd Bn.Gren.Gds. from 1st Bn.Welsh Gds. at A 12 d 4.6.
   "   11th 2nd Bn.Cold.Gds. from 2nd Bn.Scots Gds. at A 12 c 3.0.
   "   12th 1st Bn.Irish Gds. from 1st Bn.Gren.Gds. at A 18 b 6.8.

   1st Gds.Bde.M.G.Company will take over Transport Lines of 3rd Gds.Bde.M.G.Company at B 13 b 5.5 on 12th inst., From Feb: 9th to Feb: 12th 1st Gds.Bde.M.G.Company will share these Transport Lines with 3rd Gds.Bde.M.G.Company.

6. Battalion reserves of tools, S.A.A. etc. will be handed in to the Camp Commandant's Office BILLON Camps before Units leave this area. Receipts will be obtained.

   Battalion reserves of tools, S.A.A. etc. are being taken over at MAUREPAS under Brigade arrangements.

7. Petrol Tins for supply of water will be taken over at the Transport Lines which Units are taking over from 3rd Guards Brigade.

8. Defence Schemes - Air Photographs - Secret Trench Maps and all Trench Stores will be taken over by Units moving into the line. Receipts will be given and a copy of all stores taken over kept for future reference.

(2)

9. (a) Permanent fatigue parties now being found by 1st Irish Guards will be relieved by similar parties from 2nd Guards Brigade on the afternoon of Feb: 10th.

   (b) The following permanent fatigues will be found while the Brigade is in the line and taken over from similar parties of 3rd Guards Brigade at 2 P.M. on Feb: 10th :-

	Strength.	Duty.	Reporting to.	To be found by.
(i)	2 N.C.O's 6 men.	Guard on reserve Tools:S.A.A.:etc.	Town Majors Office. MAUREPAS.	2nd Bn.C.G.
(ii)	1 N.C.O. 4 men.	To work DECAUVILLE Railway.	BARBICAN dump Railway base C 1 a 4.2.	1st Bn.I.G.
(iii)	1 N.C.O. 4 men.	-do-	BILLINGSGATE Dump Railway base U 19 a 0.2.	3rd Bn.C.G.
(iv)	1 N.C.O. 1 man.	Dump in COMBLES.	Brigade H.Q., BOIS DOUAGE.	2nd Bn.C.G.

10. Attention is drawn to G.D.252/8/4 of the 13th ult., re precautionary measures against trench feet. Units using the special wash house at MAUREPAS will supply the N.C.O. in charge with the fuel and ingredients for the soap the day before they use the Baths.

11. Completion of all movements mentioned in attached table will be reported to this Office by BAB Code.

12. Brigade H.Q., will close at BILLON and open at BOIS DOUAGE - B 4 c 2.2 - at 3 P.M. on Feb: 11th.

   ACKNOWLEDGE.

   Captain,
   Brigade Major, 1st Guards Brigade.

Issued through Signals at 2 p.m.

Copy No. 1 2nd Bn. Grenadier Gds.
     2 2nd Bn. Coldstream Gds.
     3 3rd Bn. Coldstream Gds.
     4 1st Bn. Irish Gds.
     5 Bde. Machine Gun Coy.,
     6 1st Guards T.M. Battery.
     7 Guards Division.
     8 2nd Guards Brigade.
     9 3rd Guards Brigade.
Copy No. 10 75th Field Coy., R.E.
     11 1st Gds. Bde. Supply Officer.
     12 1st Gds. Bde. Transport Officer.
     13 Camp Commandant BILLON.
     14 "   "   "   MAUREPAS.
     15 O.C., Signals.
     16 Staff Captain.
     17 - 20 Retained.

March Table to be attached to 1st Guards Brigade Order No.100.

Date.	Unit.	From.	To.	Route.	Remarks.
Feb. 9th.	3/Cold.Gds.	Camp 107.	MAUREPAS.	MARICOURT - HARDECOURT.	(a) To clear BILLON Camp by 8-30 A.M. (b) 2 Lorries to be at entrance to Camp 107 at 7 A.M.
"	1st Gds.Bde. H.G.Company & T.M.Battery.	Camp 16.	MAUREPAS.	"	(a) To clear BILLON Camp by 9 A.M. but not to move before 8-30 A.M. (b) 2 Lorries to be at entrance to Camp 107 at 7 A.M.
Feb.10th.	2/Gren.Gds.	Camp 107.	MAUREPAS.	"	(a) To clear BILLON Camp by 8-30 A.M. (b) 2 Lorries to be at entrance to Camp 107 at 7 A.M.
"	3/Cold.Gds.	MAUREPAS.	Left Sub-sector. *relieving 1/Cold Gds*	MAUREPAS - FRESICOURT.	(a) Guides will be at the Dump at 24 b 9.1 at 7 P.M. Leading platoon will not pass this point before that hour.
"	1st Gds.Bde. M.G.Coy & T.M.Bty.	MAUREPAS.	Line.	MAUREPAS.	Arrangements direct.
Feb.11th.	2/Gren.Gds.	MAUREPAS.	Right Sub-sector. *relieving 1/Gren Gds*	MAUREPAS PRIEZ Farm.	(a) Guides will be at PRIEZ Farm at 7 P.M. Leading platoon will not pass this point before that hour.
"	2/Cold.Gds.	PRIEZ Farm.	MAUREPAS.	"	(a) To move on relief by 2nd Irish Gds. Time unknown at present. (b) Lorries bringing 2/I.G. blankets will take back blankets of 2/CG.
"	1st Gds.Bde. Hd.Qrs.	BILLON Wood.	BOIS DOUAGE.	MARICOURT - HARDECOURT.	1 Lorry at entrance to Camp 107 at 11 AM
Feb.12th.	1/Irish Gds.	Camp 16.	MAUREPAS.	"	(a) To clear Camp by 8-30 A.M. (b) 2 Lorries to be at entrance to Camp 16 at 7 A.M.

(a) All movement will be by Coy's in file at 500 yards interval.
(b) East of MAUREPAS all movement will be by platoons at 200 yards interval.

S E C R E T.   1st Guards Bde. No. 1514.

309/A

2nd Bn. Coldstream Gds.
2nd Guards Bde. (For information).
3rd Guards Bde. (For information).
Town Major, MAUREPAS. (For information).

       Reference March Table attached 1st Guards Bde. Order No. 100.

       2nd Bn. Coldstream Gds. will clear PRIEZ Farm at 12 noon on Feb. 11th, and not as stated on the above mentioned Order.

       2nd Bn. Irish Gds. are marching to PRIEZ Farm, and are due to clear VILLE at 8 a.m. on Feb. 11th.

                                             Captain,

8th February 1917.   Brigade Major, 1st Guards Brigade.

312

1st Guards Brigade - Intelligence Report.

OPERATIONS. - Nil.

INTELLIGENCE.   Owing to ground mist, especially in the lower country in front of us, observation was difficult. Very little movement was seen in the German lines. From U 20 c 6.6 at a true bearing of 142° men were seen carrying sandbags full of soil from some dugouts, and emptying them - Several times during the afternoon men were seen to enter and leave the dugouts.
In front of the left Battalion at about 11 P.M. the enemy were sending up a great number of red Very Lights. At the time they were shelling HEILLY POST and the ground to the North of this and the lights appeared to be a signal to "lengthen range".
Further North the enemy sent up red flares which broke into 4 or 5 red stars.   There was no apparent result.

AIRCRAFT.   Extremely active throughout the day over the left Battalion. Between 10-30 and 11-15 A.M. two hostile machines were flying very low over the left front and support lines.   It would appear that they were too low to be seen by the anti-aircraft gunners.   Lewis and Machine Gun fire was opened on the Machines which had streamers similar to our Contact Patrol Machines and which appeared to have an entirely encased fuselage.

ARTILLERY.   HEILLY and the posts on the left were shelled during the night by Field Guns from the direction of LE MESNIL.   The shooting seemed to be very erratic.   Two or three salvoes fell between HEILLY Post and the front line.
From about 6-45 A.M. to 7-45 A.M. enemy heavily shelled U 14 c 100 yards N. of CRUCIFORM POST B. H/ 4. with 4.2's
Otherwise very little artillery activity during the 24 hours.

12/2/1917.

Captain,
for Brigade Major, 1st Guards Brigade.

1st Guards Brigade - Intelligence Report.

OPERATIONS.   Nil.

INTELLIGENCE.   In front of the Left Battalion the enemy were again very active on the dugouts reported yesterday. This is probably some H.Q. previously reported on. Men were again seen continually coming and going. There appears to be two notice boards here. The exact position has not yet been verified.
   At dusk the enemy fired a few short bursts of machine gun fire across our posts, two guns being in action.
   At about 9 a.m. two rifle shots were fired at post 15 from U.20.d. central. There was a good deal of movement during the day in REUSS TRENCH at about U.20.d. An Officer came to a post or O.P. and stood for some time looking at our posts. Enemy were seen in several places looking over their parapet in this trench.
   At about 1.30 p.m. three Germans stood up on the parapet and one waved a bottle at our men and made signs inviting them to come over. On the Right Battalion front, opposite the three Advanced Posts of Right F Company, the enemy tried to fraternise and show themselves, and shout greetings in English. This, however, was stopped, as fire was opened whenever a target showed.
   It is thought probable that there is a Trench Mortar opposite No. 4 Post (U.26.c.9.9. approximate).
   An enemy wiring party was at work opposite No. 2 Post during the night.

ARTILLERY.   The hostile artillery activity during the day was slight and intermittent.
   Our Heavies appeared to be registering on the enemy trenches at about 12.30 p.m. Several shells were blind.

AIRCRAFT.   Nil.

                                                      Captain,
13/2/17.   for Brigade Major, 1st Guards Brigade.

1st Guards Brigade - Intelligence Report.

8.0 a.m. Feb. 13th to 8.30 a.m. Feb. 14th.

OPERATIONS.

Report by 1st Guards M.G. Coy., on indirect barrage fire carried out yesterday, follows immediately.

INTELLIGENCE.

The N.C.O. of No. 1 A.P. reports that on the morning of the 13th a German in opposite trench stood up for a moment with a bottle in his hand and shouted "cigarettes", evidently wishing to fraternise. The N.C.O. states that he believes the number of the German's uniform to have been 157.

An Officer in No. 3 Post reports that at 5.30 p.m. on the 13th he observed a lamp about 1800 yards to his front signalling, presumably to the front line. Following was read by Morse Code:-
"aa aa aa. K.T.E.K.U.C." Lamp then went out.

Dugouts that have been reported by our Left Battalion, and which appear to be some H.Q., were pointed out to the F.O.O., who registered his guns on them. His map reading of them is U.27.c.8.8. A compass bearing on them makes them a little more East.

Much work was going on here during the day and digging was in progress in a trench running into the big mound.

German Officers were seen several times near this. Twice Officers were seen scrutinising our lines through field-glasses.

About 6.45 a.m. Germans in full marching order came along and disappeared into a trench near by. About 7.15 more Germans, also in full marching order were seen filing out of the trench, and disappearing over the hill crest.

5 Officers and 3 Orderlies came along to their front line and spoke to the sentries - U.20.a. These sentries can be easily seen by us - they appear to be relieved every hour.

Lights - Enemy used many different lights during the past 24 hours. It was again observed that he used red lights when his shells fell near his own lines. Green lights were also frequently used. A light breaking into two reds and a green appeared to be the signal for a barrage in and behind SAILLESEL soon after dark.

AIRCRAFT.

Very active throughout the day. Two planes cruised at a low altitude over the front line from 10.30 - 12 noon. They were twice driven off by our de Havilands.

At 3.30 p.m. a plane was hit by our anti-aircraft gun, and crashed in front of the Reserve line.

At 4.40 p.m. five enemy planes flew over the line - a white light was dropped by one of them and they immediately returned across their own lines.

ARTILLERY. - Fairly active throughout the day in Left Batt. area. Retaliation for our bombardment was not very severe on our front, but the left posts and Reilly Post were rather severely shelled.

The following Artillery tests were carried out by Right Front Battalion:-

		Message sent.	Result.
Test (a)	Right Front Coy.	2.17	2.19½
	Left Front Coy.	12.45	12.47
Test (b)	(O.C. Batt. Call).	5.45 p.m.	5.47½

signature

Captain,

14th February 1917.   Brigade Major, 1st Guards Bde.

During the shoot yesterday afternoon by the 1st Guards M.G. Coy., 20,000 rounds were fired on RHINE TRENCH and 2,000 rounds on ISOLDE ALLEY.

During the last 10 minutes of the shoot the 5 guns firing on RHINE TRENCH were evidently spotted by hostile aircraft, as the ground in the immediate vicinity was searched by 5.9's.

RHINE TRENCH guns being in the open were easily spotted, whilst the 2 guns firing on ISOLDE ALLEY drew no fire.

1st Guards Brigade - Intelligence Report.

8 A.M. Feb: 14th to 8 A.M. Feb: 15th.

OPERATIONS. Patrols were sent out by left front Company of Right Battalion to reconnoitre saps and German wire from U 26 a 6.6 - U 26 a 7.0. i.e. opposite posts 5, 6, 8, 9.
<u>Opposite No. 5 Post.</u> German wire is about 20 yards from ours. Condition, moderate, consisting of old French wire with barbed wire among it. A party could be heard working under ridge behind wire. German wire appeared to be continuous but weak.
<u>Opposite No. 6 Post.</u> Sap or advanced post was located about 80 yards from our wire. Very Lights were continuously fired from here. German wire can be seen on top of crest behind this sap and work could be heard.
<u>Opposite No. 8 Post.</u> German wire encountered about 60 yards from our wire. It is better on right than left, consisting on former of new concertina wire, on latter of old wire on stakes.
<u>Opposite No. 9 Post.</u> Sap located 60 yards from our wire. Its head can be clearly made out by an iron post about 4 ft. high on a small mound. Patrol could not see any wire, as ground drops very quickly behind sap.
Patrols throughout found difficulty in getting through our wire, which is fairly strong.

From the Left Battn. several listening posts went out. The Germans could be heard working in their trench but nothing was seen.

INTELLIGENCE. At about 6-45 A.M. an enemy fatigue party of about 10 men was seen from the right Battn. bringing camp kettles from a large dugout about 500 yards in front of F.2., to the enemy's front line.
From about 6-30 to 7 A.M. enemy fired rifle grenades at F.2 and 3 from a position 26 d 1.9. Our 18 pdr. retaliated with 20 rounds on "S.O.S." line.
From the left Battn. much movement was again observed during the day at the dugouts reported yesterday. The dugouts are in or near LARGE Trench (U 26 b 7.0.).
At 8-45 A.M. a German was seen running out a telephone wire to the left of the mound.
There is a small red and white triangular flag outside what appears to be a dugout at U 20 d 3.6.

AIRCRAFT. Hostile Aircraft very active during most of the day. Several of the Machines were flying very low and one fired at the Reserve Line with his Machine Gun - 1 man was hit. Lewis Gun fire was kept up on them.
One enemy Machine was marked with two black bars upon the lower wings.

ARTILLERY. There was intermittent hostile shelling during the day. At 12-25 P.M. a heavy barrage was opened on SAILLISEL.
At 7-30 P.M. the enemy commenced a fairly heavy shelling with shrapnel and 5-9's from posts F.1 and F.2 along the BAPAUME Road to the Reserve Line and also on the DECAUVILLE behind the reserve line. Telephone line and DECAUVILLE Railway were broken in places. The shelling lasted for half an hour.
From 9 P.M. to 9-30 P.M. enemy Field Guns opened bursts of fire on the left front posts. The bursts were followed by yellow flares bursting into 3 red stars. These were probably a signal to lengthen range.

Captain,
Brigade Major, 1st Guards Brigade.

Intelligence Report - 1st Guards Brigade.

8 A.M. Feb: 15th to 8 A.M. Feb: 16th.

OPERATIONS.

A patrol went out from No.15 Advanced Post at 12 midnight returning at 2 A.M. The patrol was instructed to lie out and listen and in particular to observe whether there were any advanced posts in front of the German line - No such Posts were found. Germans could be heard talking in their trench but none were seen moving outside.

INTELLIGENCE.

A German Officer and Orderly were seen to leave LARCH Trench 50 yards N.E. of the Mounds at U 26 b 7.0. and walk back into the thick part of the Wood. He returned shortly afterwards and entered the Trench at the same place.

An enemy Machine Gun 600 yards behind the German line opposite our Left Battalion fired at a low flying aeroplane of ours at about 4 P.M.

In front of the Right Battalion the enemy fired a Red Very Light from their front line towards the rear - this was immediately answered by a similar light being fired from the Support line towards the Front.

At 4-30 A.M. the enemy fired a Green light. No action followed.

An enemy Machine Gun has been located South of the new Chalk Trench, called HIENRICH Trench.

AIRCRAFT.

From the right Battalion a B.E.2 E Machine was reported to be fighting two enemy Machines, when its tail came off and it was seen to crash to ground on HILL 150.

At 5-45 P.M. a hostile Machine passed over BLAMONT Reserve line firing a considerable number of Tracer bullets at the Duckwalk and DACAUVILLE Railway - No damage was done.

The Lewis Guns of the Left Battalion were continually in action against hostile Aircraft during the day. Two hostile Machines with Streamers again flew very low over our line and were fired upon.

ARTILLERY.

A heavy barrage of H.E. was put down on Advanced Posts 1 - 4, S.1. and S.2., S.6 - 8. before the relief of the right Battalion took place. No damage was done.

From 10-30 to 11 A.M. the enemy continuously shelled the main Road in the left Battn's Sector with 77 m.m.

In retaliation to our bombardment the enemy shelled SINISTER and No. 8 Post from 4-15 to 5 P.M. with a few bursts of 77 m.m.

At 5-30 P.M. the enemy sent up White lights bursting into Red Stars from SAILLISEL and Southwards to our front. This was immediately followed by a heavy barrage upon the former place and a lighter one upon our line. The points chiefly shelled were SINISTER and the right of RIGHT BAR. The barrage which lasted for 15 minutes caused no damage.

MACHINE GUNS.

200 rounds were fired by our Guns at K.1. and L.1. A new Gun has been placed as ordered in BISHOP'S AVENUE - 25 b 8½.7.

Captain,
Brigade Major, 1st Guards Brigade.

Intelligence Report - 1st Guards Brigade.

8 A.M. Feb: 16th - 8 A.M. Feb: 17th.

OPERATIONS.

The following patrols went out from our Posts :-

No. 6 Post - A patrol of 1 N.C.O. and 2 men went out at 8 P.M. for the purpose of reconnoitring the enemy sap heads and wire. A German bombing sap was found about 100 yards in front of our line. The nature of the ground to the sap is rough and about 14 yards in front of it there is a wire entanglement of concertina wire about 4 yards in depth. The sap is of a horse-shoe shape and is connected by a battered C.T. to another sap, the occupants of which seem to be observing our line at No. 9 Post. No trenches were seen in rear of these two Saps and it was not possible to estimate the number of enemy occupying them. The patrol returned at 8-35 P.M.

No. 9 Post - A patrol of 1 N.C.O. and 1 man went out for a similar purpose as above. They found the German sap to be 180 yards to the left front of their post - the sap really was found to consist of two portions, one larger one joining a smaller and forming a curve. The sap appeared to be about 3ft. deep and very thinly wired with many gaps. An old battered trench connected this sap with the sap opposite No. 6 Post which is about 100 yards to the right.

No. 17 Post- A listening patrol went out from No.17 Post for 3/4 of an hour - There was nothing to report.

No. 19 Post- A listening patrol went out at 1 A.M. They heard the enemy talking and digging. The sap opposite No. 20 Post is occupied by the enemy.

A deserter came over to post 20 during the early part of the night, he carried no Arms or equipment and when he was seen and spoken to by an Officer he came in quietly.

He confirms the presence of two Battalion H.Q., in the MOUNDS in ST. PIERRE VAAST WOOD and of Reserve Battalion H.Q., in the QUARRY South of GOVERNMENT FARM.

An Officer went out to locate the exact position of the above MOUNDS and found them to be at U 26 b 8.5. and U 26 b 5.9.

INTELLIGENCE.

Six Rifle Grenades were fired by the enemy at 7 A.M. on the 16th. They fell behind No. 2 Post. At 8-30 A.M. enemy were heard working on their front line opposite this Post. The sound of iron being hammered was heard and lasted for 20 minutes. About the same time small parties of the enemy were seen in ST. PIERRE VAAST WOOD opposite A.P. 1 and 2.. The enemy were also seen working on their front line opposite Post No. 5.

Between 10 and 11 A.M. the enemy were registering and several rounds were seen to fall short into their own line. Red flares were sent up and the range was immediately lengthened.

During the day a party of the enemy were seen wearing a new type of cap. The shape was very similar to the Service Dress Cap without a peak and not like the "Feldmutze".

Wheeled traffic was heard from A.A.P.3 at 5-45 P.M. on the 16th in a S.E. direction. During the day enemy made signs and were talking in the direction of our Advanced Posts evidently wishing to fraternise.

From the Left Battalion a party of the enemy were observed to be working on the MOUNDS from 6-50 to 9 A.M. Men were continually seen walking down the road which runs N.E. through ST. PIERRE VAAST WOOD.

A net-work of overhead wires, probably camouflage, was observed South of the Mound at U.26 b 8.5.

AIRCRAFT.
A considerable number of our Machines were in the air yesterday. Hostile Machines were again flying low over the Right Battalion and were continually fired at by our Lewis Guns. No duels took place.

ARTILLERY.
A.P.2 and 3 report that a horn was blown in the German lines when our guns made a direct hit on their line. Hostile Artillery activity was slight on the left Battalion front. A few 77 mm. shells were fired at No.15 Post, the duck-boards in front of RIGHT BAR Support Post and at the BAPAUME - PERONNE Road.

MACHINE GUNS.
The M.G. at BISHOP's AVENUE and the Guns at Company H.Q., fired about 100 rounds each at hostile Aircraft.

Clarkson
Captain,
for Brigade Major, 1st Guards Brigade.

1st Guards Brigade - Intelligence Report.

8 A.M. Feb: 17th to 8 A.M. Feb: 18th.

OPERATIONS.

    Patrols - Owing to the thaw and the rain quiet movement was impossible and the shell holes being full of water afforded no cover.

    No.1 A.Adv.Post.- Patrol of 1 N.C.O. and 2 men went out at 12-10 A.M. They worked along an old trench in front of the German line, where they heard plenty of talking and one man moving about in the trench sounded muddy.

    No.2 Adv. Post. - A similar patrol left this post and reached the German wire which they found to be 60 yds. distant from our Post. No movement was heard.

    No.3 Adv. Post - Similar patrol left this Post and reported the German wire to be in fairly good condition. Again no movement in the enemy's line was heard.

    No.5 Post - A similar party left this Post between 1 A.M. and 1-30 A.M. They reached the German wire and report that a wiring party was working on it.

    No.7 Post - A similar patrol which left this Post report that they heard a party of the enemy working in front of his Post.

    No.9 Post - A similar patrol went out at 3 A.M. They report having reached a sap which was found to be in a battered condition and badly wired.

    No.14 Post - An Officers patrol went out at 1-30 A.M. Nothing could be heard in the German Line. The patrol came across the wire just below the crest. As far as could be seen there was no other line of wire in rear of this, but owing to the small number of Very Lights sent up observation was difficult.

    No.19 Post - An Officers patrol went out at 2-15 A.M. and proceeded to U 20 d 2.5. Very few Very Lights were sent up and no sound of talking or knocking could be heard. One thin line of German wire was found and no other line in rear of this could be seen. The ground leading up to the enemy's line was very much cut up by shell fire. It was considered very unusual that nothing was heard during the two hours the patrol was out, as the sound of talking in the German line is generally quite audible from our Post.

INTELLIGENCE.

    At about 5-30 A.M. when the enemy were putting down a fairly heavy bombardment on the right of the right front Coy. the enemy fired red flares breaking into two red stars and signalling with a red lamp was also observed in ST. PIERRE VAAST WOOD.

    At this time from the left Battn/ front mens with rifles and packs were observed at about U 26 a 7.8. moving East.

AIRCRAFT.

    - Nil -

ARTILLERY.

    Tests - The right front company carried out Artillery tests at 10-35 A.M. in U.26.2. The message was despatched 10-35 and the first shell passed over at 10-37. The fog prevented observation.

    On the left Battalion front a test was carried out in U.20.2. The message was despatched at 2-30 P.M. and the first shell passed over at 2-31 P.M.

    On the right Battalion front from 5-40 A.M. to 6-10 A.M. the enemy shelled the front and support lines with 4'2,s and 5.9's. Most of the shells fell on the extreme right of the Battalion frontage.

    On the left Battalion front the Artillery activity was considerably below normal. At about 4 P.M. RIGHT BAR No. 6 was shelled for about 5 minutes and a few small shells were fired on the Posts at 1-15 A.M. and 5-45 A.M.

MACHINE GUNS.

During the night the Guns of K.2. and K.3. fired 2,200 rounds from improvised positions at U 25 a 9½.7. at the German communications in U 21 C. and D. Both Traversing and Vertical Searching fire were used.

Clarkson Captain,
Brigade Major, 1st Guards Brigade.

1st Guards Brigade - Intelligence Report.

8 A.M. Feb: 18th to 8 A.M. Feb: 19th.

OPERATIONS.

Patrols - 8 Patrols each consisting of 1 N.C.O. and 2 men went out from the Right Battalion Posts between the hours 9 P.M. and 3-30 A.M. Opposite A.P. 1 wire was found to be very good, but it got weaker opposite A.P. 2. Two passages or gaps through it were found.
Opposite the other Posts the Patrols heard the sound of the enemy working and baling out his trenches.
The ground between the lines was very muddy and rough. The patrols came across several dis-used trenches and a good deal of loose wire.

Sniping - A German who came out in front of his Post, apparently with the object of digging, was killed by a sniper from No. 14 Post.

INTELLIGENCE.

During the course of the morning odd parties of Germans were seen moving about in their lines but owing to the mist observation was very difficult.
From the left Battalion movement was observed in the vicinity of the Mounds, which has been previously reported upon.
The enemy were extremely quiet during the night and practically no Lights were sent up opposite our Posts.

AIRCRAFT.

Nil.

ARTILLERY.

There was very little Artillery activity throughout the day or night. At about 3 P.M. a few 77 mm. and 4.2" shells fell behind No. 7 Post.
A working party in the support trench of the Left Battalion drew a little fire.

MACHINE GUNS.

About 1,000 rounds were fired during the night by K.2. and K.3.
ISOLDE Alley and targets in U 21 c. and d. were searched with indirect fire.

Captain,
for Brigade Major, 1st Guards Brigade.

1st Guards Brigade Intelligence Report.

8 A.M. Feb: 19th to 8 A.M. Feb: 20th.

OPERATIONS.

Patrols - An Officers patrol went out from No.20 Post at 11 P.M. with the idea of finding out how strongly the Post at U 20 d 4.7. was held. Owing to the heavy state of the ground and to the fact that our guns were firing on their barrage lines the object was not attained.
    An enemy working party was heard digging in the vicinity of RING Trench.
    Another Officers patrol went out from No. 15 Post at 12-30 A.M. with a view to obtaining information about the "Blockhouse" near U 20 d 0.1. The enemy wire was found to consist of a mixture of French and Strand, 2ft. 6" in height and not very deep. Talking and coughing could be heard but there was no sound of work in progress.

Sniping - A sniper firing from about U 20 a 6.6. hit an Officer who exposed himself behind No. 12 Post. This was the only Rifle shot fired during the day. No attempt was made to fire on the men who came to his aid.

INTELLIGENCE.

Much new work has been done by the enemy in the past four days - especially in TROLL and HEINRICH trenches.
    The left Battalion report that compass bearings taken on the large MOUNDS, previously mentioned, do not tally with any of the M.G., shown on the Map framed on the information from the prisoner taken in the Sector.
    A good deal of movement was seen near STRAUSS Trench. Our Artillery fired on targets in this vicinity.
    Owing to the mist observation was very difficult, but it appeared that a party of about 20 men opposite Post 6 were wearing dark Green Uniform with steel helmets and a white band round the left shoulder. At about 9-30 P.M. the sound of a relief taking place was heard opposite F.E.

AIRCRAFT.

NIL.

ARTILLERY.

Opposite the right Battalion at 3 P.M. the enemy shelled his own line. Red Very Lights were sent up and the shelling ceased. Shortly after this a few 4.2"s were sent over our front line.
    Artillery Test carried out at 3 P.M. First shell went over 20 seconds later and the fifth shell 40 seconds later.
    On the left Battalion front the enemy shelled the vicinity of RIGHT BAR throughout the day. The shells appeared to be coming from the direction of the Northern part of ST. MARTIN WOOD. Otherwise Artillery activity below normal.

MACHINE GUNS.

A short burst of hostile Machine Gun fire was turned on to the right Support of the left Battalion. This Gun probably fires from TROLL Support. It fires over the Road at U 20 c 3.0. which is very visible to the enemy and gives them a skyline target.
    1050 rounds of indirect fire was carried out by K.2. and K.3. Guns last night, the target being U 22 c 3.5. where FARM Trench enters ST. PIERRE VAAST WOOD.

[signature] Captain,
for Brigade Major, 1st Guards Brigade.

1st Guards Brigade Intelligence Report.
----
8 A.M. Feb: 20th to 8 A.M. Feb: 21st.

OPERATIONS.

Patrols - On Officers patrol went out from Post 20 at 10 P.M. to ascertain how strongly the enemy's Posts were held. The Patrol passed about 30 yards North of the enemy's sap where the wire is tall and strong. They remained for about half-an-hour in front of enemy wire. From sounds and indications the line seems more strongly held than was reported by the deserter. Enemy were hard at work wiring - On the left bombing took place, and a German shouted out "Kamerad" very loud 3 times.

INTELLIGENCE.

During night of 19th/20th enemy were heard working opposite A.P.3. Fresh earth was seen in morning.

The German sentries appear to be on duty from 2 to 3 hours and they hand over their steel-helmet when taking over.

Enemy were observed signalling with lamp on right of GOVERNMENT FARM at 6 A.M. on morning of 20th.

White Lights were observed to be sent up by Germans opposite No. 8 Post. These were repeated twice, getting further back each time.

Opposite No. 10 Post enemy were seen to be baling water out of trenches.

Opposite the Left Battalion the enemy was seen baling water out of his front line and a pump was at work during most of the day.

There is a large dugout in BEECH LANE, where movement is going on all day, a compass bearing would put it at U 26 d 25.65. but this reading will be verified later.

Small parties of the enemy were seen working on or near TRISTAN Trench.

A telephone wire is being run out from HEINRICH Trench at about U 26 b 3.9.

Several Very Lights were fired from the enemy front line between 7 and 9 A.M.: there was no apparent result.

AIRCRAFT.   NIL.

ARTILLERY.

On the right Battalion front the duckboards leading up to the front line from BLAMONT Reserve were frequently shelled with 77 mm. during the day.

At about 3-30 P.M. No(s. 2, 3 Posts of the left Reserve Company were shelled by Field Guns and 4.5's. No damage was done.

On the left Battalion front the enemy obtained direct hits with one 77 mm. shell each upon No. 8 Post and upon the entrance to the dugout in the ORCHARD.

MACHINE GUNS.

During the night K.2. and K.3. Guns again fired about 1250 rounds upon the German tracks and trenches at U 22 c 3.5.

Captain,
for Brigade Major, 1st Guards Brigade.

1st Guards Brigade - Intelligence Report.

8 A.M. Feb: 21st to 8 A.M. Feb: 22nd.

OPERATIONS. Nil.

INTELLIGENCE.

The light was extremely bad for observation. From the left Battalion the usual movement was observed in HEINRICH and TROLL Trenches.

New enemy wire has been put out in front of RAUSS Trench U 20 c 8.2.

The Mound at U 26 b 2.1. is frequently used. The position of this place needs verifying, but it appears to be joined by a shallow trench to the Mound U 26 b 8.5. From this position the enemy gets a view of all our Posts and presumeably of the high ground South of SAILLISEL.

The Blockhouse at U 20 d 1.1. has a small red flag flying just outside what appears to be an entrance to a dugout.

A listening post was sent out after midnight from U 20 d 1/2. 8 1/2. in front of No. 20 Post. An enemy working party was heard about U 20 d 3.6. There was much talking and coughing.

On the right Battalion front the day passed quietly until 6 P.M. A good deal of work was done under cover of the mist.

AIRCRAFT. Nil.

ARTILLERY.

At 6 P.M. the enemy put down a heavy barrage on the left of the left Battalion and on the ground to the North. This lasted for about half-an-hour. It was preceded by a great display of red lights fired from the front line and answered from the rear.

On the right Battalion front the barrage rapidly moved South until it covered the BAPAUME Road and duck:boards.

MACHINE GUNS.

Indirect fire was again used during the night, the K.2. and K.3. Guns firing 1,500 rounds on four different targets in U 21 c and d and FARM Trench in U 22 c.

Captain,
for Brigade Major, 1st Guards Brigade.

1st Guards Brigade Intelligence Report.

8 A.M. Feb: 22nd to 8 A.M. Feb: 23rd.

OPERATIONS.

Patrols - From the right Battalion a patrol went out from No. 1 Post to establish communication with the Battalion on the right.

From the left Battalion four listening Patrols went out -

Post 14 - Patrol remained out from 3 to 5 A.M. in front of the German wire.

No. 17 Post - Patrol remained out from 12 midnight to 5 A.M.

No. 21 Post - A patrol went out about 50 yards from our wire and remained out for 4 hours.

No. 22 Post - Patrol left this Post at U.20. and proceeded 60 yards towards U.20.4. where they lay outside the German wire for one and a half hours.

None of the above patrols heard any sounds of relief. Coughing and talking were audible and one German was seen dragging something along the ground outside his wire. He was probably wiring.

INTELLIGENCE.

New work is observed at U 26 b 0.3. approximate. Much smoke was seen here during the day.

The enemy were very quiet before 2 P.M. in front of the right flank Company. From 2 to 4 P.M. a few Rifle Grenades or light Trench Mortar Bombs were fired without effect towards S.1.

From the left Battalion Officers were seen studying our lines with glasses from U 26 b 8.5. Two of them had Maps, they eventually disappeared into the Mound.

AIRCRAFT.

Nil.

ARTILLERY.

Activity very much below normal. A few shells were fired by the enemy at 4.10 P.M. at the front Posts of the Left Batt, one or two of these fell into the enemy wire and the usual red Rocket was sent up, which was answered by another from somewhere inside the Wood and finally by one much further back.

MACHINE GUNS.

2,300 rounds of indirect fire were fired between 12 midnight and 4 A.M. by our Machine Guns on German tracks and trenches South of ISOLDE Alley (U 21 d), all approached West of WOOD Lane (U 22 c) and FARM Trench (U 22 c).

for Brigade Major, 1st Guards Brigade. Captain,

1st Guards Brigade Intelligence Report.

8 A.M. Feb: 23rd to 8 A.M. Feb: 24th.

OPERATIONS.

Patrols - Listening Patrols were sent out from Posts 5 - 10. An Officer accompanied the patrol from No. 6 Post. They lay out about 20 yards in front of our wire and report sounds of hammering and pumping as being heard in the enemy's line along the edge of ST. PIERRE VAAST WOOD U 26 a 8.3, to U 26 a 4.4, opposite the Posts 8, 9 and 10.

An Officers patrol went out from Post 15 at 7-15 P.M. with the object of reconnoitring the supposed German sap opposite No's 13 and 14 Posts. The patrol moved on a compass bearing of 145° and the German wire was reached after about 100 yards. It was found to be thick and in good condition. Turning to the South the patrol reconnoitred the German wire and found a gap opposite our No. 14 Post. From inside the wire a continuous line of parapet was observed and the German Posts were consequently difficult to locate. From the sound of coughing however, a German Post is suspected as being slightly to the South of a point opposite our No. 15 Post, and three more Posts opposite our No's 13 and 14.

The German wire was followed for about 120 yards. Patrol then turned West and re-entered our line at No. 13 Post at 8-50 P.M. The German wire was 75 yards distant from our No. 12 Post.

Listening Patrols were put out in front of No. 15 and 17 Posts and remained out all night. No enemy movement was observed.

Two patrols left No. 20 Post at 7 P.M; and 1 A.M. respectively with instructions to proceed to the German wire opposite the German Post at U 20.4. Both patrols reached the German wire, remaining out for one- and a half hours each, but no movement was observed. Coughing and talking were heard.

INTELLIGENCE.

At 12-40 P.M. small enemy working parties were observed at different places in the vicinity of the Mound at U 26 b 8.5. The fog prevented further observation.

AIRCRAFT.

Nil.

ARTILLERY.

At about 10-30 A.M. our No. 5 Reserve Post (M.G.) was slightly shelled by enemy Howitzers.

At 2 P.M. our Artillery fired upon the Blockhouse U 30 d 0.1. From No. 7 Post trench boards were observed flying through the air.

At about 8 P.M. heavy Artillery fire to the South spread to our right Battalion. At about 8-15 P.M. the enemy sent up red rockets from the front line. This was immediately followed by a brisk barrage of shrapnel, 77 mm. and 4.2's. The points most heavily shelled were A P 1, S 1, F 3, F 4, Posts 8, 9 and 10, the BAPAUME Road and about 50 yards to the right of S 3. A few shells fell in rear of the reserve line at about R 3. Firing ceased at about 8-45 P.M.

The above barrage spread to the left Battalion Front, Support and reserve lines, inflicting no damage. A large number of blind shells were observed.

MACHINE GUNS.

Hostile Machine Guns employed indirect fire from the direction of U 21 a 4.5. at a long range against the Support line of the left Battalion. Another Machine Gun fired two bursts which passed over CRUCIFORM Post, the Reserve line and hit the Decauville at left Battalion H.Q.

Clarkson Captain,
for Brigade Major, 1st Guards Brigade.

SECRET.   Copy No. 22

1st Guards Brigade Order No. 101.

Ref. Map - ALBERT Combined Sheet 1/40,000.   Feb: 23rd, 1917.

1. The 1st Guards Brigade will be relieved in the FREGICOURT Sector on Feb: 26th and 27th in accordance with attached Table. Further details od relief will be arranged direct between Units concerned.

2. Details of relief of M. G. Coy's. and T. M. Bty's. will be arranged direct between O. C's concerned.

3. Until 3 P.M. on Feb: 27th, Units of 2nd Guards Brigade on arrival in the forward area will come under the tactical Command of G.O.C., 1st Guards Brigade.
   Similarly Units of 1st Guards Brigade on arrival in the BILLON Camps area will come under the tactical Command of G.O.C., 2nd Guards Brigade.
   The 2nd Bn. Coldstream Guards on arrival at VILLE will come under the tactical Command of G.O.C., 3rd Guards Brigade and will form part of the Corps Reserve.

4. Billeting parties of Units moving into BILLON Camps will be sent forward in advance and will report to the Camp Commdt. at 8 A.M. on the day on which their Unit moves in.
   Arrangements for the transport of billeting party of 2nd Bn. Coldstream Guards will be notified later.

5. (a) 1st Line Transport will move in rear of Units. An interval of not less than 200 yards will be left between every 4 vehicles.

   (b) Transport Lines are being taken over as follows :-

        2/Irish Gds. from 3/Cold.Gds.
        3/Gren Gds.   "   2/Gren.Gds.
        1/Cold.Gds.   "   2/Cold.Gds.
        1/Scots Gds. "   1/Irish Gds.

6. Petrol Tins will be handed over in the Transport Lines. Special care will be taken by Battn's. coming out of the Line to send their empty Tins back to their Transport Lines before they leave the forward area.

7. (a) The following fatigues will be relieved at 2 P.M. on Feb: 26th by similar parties from 2nd Guards Brigade :-

   (i)   The Guard on Reserve S.A.A. and bombs at MAUREPAS.
   (ii) The 1 N.C.O. and 4 men working each of the Decauville Rly's.
   (iii) The 1 N.C.O. and 1 man on the Pump in COMBLES.
         The 2nd Bn. Coldstream Guards will arrange to have a guide at Brigade H.Q., by 2 P.M. on 27th. for (iii).

   (b) The 2nd Bn. Grenadier Guards and 3rd Bn. Coldstream Guards will each find 1 Company to take over the BRIQUETERIE fatigue. These Coy's. will move under Battn. arrangements so as to arrive at the BRIQUETERIE at 3 P.M. on Feb: 27th. They will be rationed by the S.S.O., from Feb: 28th inclusive.

1.

2.

8. Regimental Reserves of S.A.A. and bombs will be taken and handed over under Brigade arrangements. Tools will not be dumped.

9. Defence Schemes – air photographs – secret trench maps, and all trench stores, will be handed over by Units in the line, to relieving Units.
2nd Bn. Grenadier Gds. and 3rd Bn. Coldstream Gds. will send in any of the above in their possession to Brigade H.Q. before they leave the forward area.

10. Completion of all movements will be reported to this Office.

11. Brigade H.Q. will close at BOIS DOUAGE and open at BILLON WOOD at 3 P.M. on February 27th.

ACKNOWLEDGE.

Issued at 8-30 p.m.

M.B. Smith
Captain,
Brigade Major, 1st Guards Bde.

Copy No.	1	to	2nd Bn. Grenadier Gds.	Copy No.	11	to	Right Bde.
"	"	2	"	2nd Bn. Coldstream Gds.	"	"	12	"	Right Group G.D.A.
"	"	3	"	3rd Bn. Coldstream Gds.	"	"	13	"	Left Group G.D.A.
"	"	4	"	1st Bn. Irish Gds.	"	"	14	"	75th Coy. R.E.
"	"	5	"	1st Guards M.G. Coy.	"	"	15	"	1st Guards Bde. S.O.
"	"	6	"	1st Guards T.M. Battery.	"	"	16	"	1st Gds. Bde. T.O.
"	"	7	"	Guards Division.	"	"	17	"	Camp Comdt. BILLON.
"	"	8	"	2nd Guards Bde.	"	"	18	"	Town Major, MAUREPAS.
"	"	9	"	3rd Guards Bde.	"	"	19	"	Staff Captain.
"	"	10	"	Left Bde.	"	"	20	"	O.C. Signals.

MARCH TABLE.

Date.	Unit.	From.	To.	Relieved by.	Route.	Remarks.
Feb: 25th.	3/Cold.Gds.	MAUREPAS.	BILLON 107. (vacated by 2/I.G.)	2/Irish Gds.	HARDECOURT-MARICOURT.	(a) To start from Camp at 10 AM. (b) Lorries will be at entrance to Camp at Docauville Rly. Crossing at 8 AM.
26th.	2/Cold.Gds.	Left Sub-Sector.	MAUREPAS. (vacated by 2/I.G.)	2/Irish Gds.	FREGICOURT-COMBLES.	(a) An Officer of 2/I.G. will visit Bn.H.Q. on 25th to arrange details. Also 1 N.C.O. per Coy. to take over Stores - work-fatigues etc. N.C.O's will remain. (b) 1 guide per front and support line Posts & 1 guide per Platoon from Reserve Coy's. to be at BILLINGSGATE Dump at 7 PM. when 2/I.G. are due to arrive.
	2/Gren.Gds.	MAUREPAS.	BILLON 107. (vacated by 3/G.G.)	3/G.G.	HARDECOURT-MARICOURT.	(a) To start from Camp at 10 AM. (b) Lorries will be at Decauville level crossing at entrance to Camp at 8 AM.
	1st Gds.Bde. M.G.Coy. & T.M.Bty.	MAUREPAS.	Line.	2nd Gds.Bde. M.G.Coy. & T.M.Bty.	Any.	(a) In-coming troops to be clear of W. end of duckboards by 7 PM. (b) Details can be sent on to BILLON by arrangement with Camp Commandant, BILLON.
27th.	1/Irish Gds.	MAUREPAS.	Line.	3/Gren.Gds.	PRIEZ FM.	(a) An Officer of 3/G.G. will visit Bn.H.Q. on 26th to arrange details - Also 1 N.C.O. per Coy. to take over stores - work - fatigues etc. N.C.O's will remain in the Line. (b) 1 guide per front & support line Posts & 1 guide per Platoon from Reserve Coy's. to be at BARBICAN Dump at 7 PM. when 3/G.G. are due to arrive.

(2)

Date.	Unit.	From.	To.	Relieved by.	Route.	Remarks.
Feb 27th	2/Cold.Gds.	MAUREPAS.	VILLE. (vacated by 2/S.G.)	1/Scots Gds.	Rail from PLATEAU.	(a) Starting time of train and transport to be notified later. (b) Two lorries will be at entrance to MAUREPAS Camp at 3 A.M.
	1st Gds.Bde. M.G.Coy. & T.M.Bty.	MAUREPAS.	BILLON Camp 16.	—	HARDECOURT. MARICOURT.	(a) To start from Camp at 10 AM. (b) 1 lorry for M.G.Coy. & 1 for T.M.Bty. at entrance to MAUREPAS Camp Decauville level crossing at 3 A.M.
	1st Gds.Bde. Hd-Qrs.	MAUREPAS.	BILLON WOOD.	2nd Gds.Bde. Hd-Qrs.	"	1 lorry at Brigade H.Q. at 11 AM.
28th.	1/Irish Gds.	MAUREPAS.	BILLON Camp 16. (vacated by 1/C.G.)	1/Cold.Gds.	"	(a) To start from Camp at 10 AM. (b) Two lorries will be at entrance to MAUREPAS Camp at Decauville level crossing at 9 AM.

(a) All movement will be by Coy's. in file at 500 yards interval between Coy's.

(b) East of MAUREPAS all movement will be by Platoons at 200 yards interval.

1st Gds Bde.

G.D. No. 2696/5/G.

Reference foot-note Appendix 'A', Guards Division Order No. 109 - March Table is attached.

A C K N O W L E D G E .

C. Heywood
Lieut-Colonel,
General Staff. Guards Divn.

25th February 1917.

DATE.	UNIT.	FROM.	TO.	REMARKS.
Feb. ~~29th~~ 27.	2/Coldstream Gds.	MAUREPAS.	VILLE.	March to PLATEAU, thence by train leaving at 11.30 a.m. to ANCRE Junction E.21.b.10.7, thence by march route to VILLE.
	2/Scots Guards.	VILLE.	PRIEZ FM.	March to ANCRE JUNCTION, E.21.b.10.7 thence by train leaving at 9 a.m. to PLATEAU, thence by march route to PRIEZ.
	1/Scots Guards.	PRIEZ FM.	MAUREPAS.	On relief by 2/Scots Guards.

DATE.	UNIT.	FROM.	TO.	REMARKS.
Feb.29th 27	2/Coldstream Gds.	MAUREPAS.	VILLE.	March to PLATEAU, thence by train leaving at 11.30 a.m. to ANCRE Junction E.21.b.10.7, thence by march route to VILLE.
	2/Scots Guards.	VILLE.	PRIEZ FM.	March to ANCRE JUNCTION, E.21.b.10.7 thence by train leaving at 9 a.m. to PLATEAU, thence by march route to PRIEZ.
	1/Scots Guards.	PRIEZ FM.	MAUREPAS.	On relief by 2/Scots Guards.

SECRET

Copy No. 6

GUARDS DIVISION ORDER NO. 109.

1. (a) 2nd Guards Brigade will relieve 1st Guards Brigade in the line on nights of 26th/27th and 27th/28th February.

    Details of relief will be arranged between Brigades concerned.

    (b) On relief 1st Guards Brigade will move into Divisional Reserve.

    (c) 3rd Guards Brigade will remain in Corps Reserve, but will find the Battalion at PRIEZ FARM.

    (d) 76th Field Co. R.E. will relieve 75th Field Co. R.E. in the line, the latter moving on relief to BRONFAY FARM.

    55th Field Co. R.E. will move from BRONFAY FARM to MAUREPAS.

2. Movements will be carried out in accordance with Appendix 'A' attached.

    Disposition of the Division on completion of relief is shewn in Appendix 'B' attached.

3. During the process of relief G.Os.C. Guards Brigades will have under their tactical command all Battalions in their respective Brigade areas.

    The Battalion 1st Guards Brigade moving to MERICOURT will, on arrival, form part of Corps Reserve and will be under tactical command of G.O.C. 3rd Guards Brigade.

4. 1st Guards Brigade will take over the BRIQUETERIE working party from 3rd Guards Brigade, under arrangements to be made between Guards Brigades concerned.

<u>ACKNOWLEDGE</u>.

C P Hayward
Lieut-Colonel,
General Staff, Guards Divn.

22nd February 1917.

Issued to Signals at 3 p.m.

Copy No. 1 General Staff. 9 Divnl. Signals.
       2 "Q".   10 A.D.M.S.
       3 G.D.A.   11 A.D.V.S.   17. 40th Division.
       4 C.R.E.   12 A.P.M.   18. XIV Corps.
       5 1st Guards Bde.   13 Divnl. Train.   19. Camp Comdt. MAUREPAS.
       6 2nd Guards Bde.   14 S.S.O.   20. Camp Comdt. BILLON.
       7 3rd Guards Bde.   15 D.A.D.O.S.   21. Camp Comdt. BRONFAY.
       8 Pioneer Batt.   16 29th Division.   22. Town Major MERICOURT.
                                                23. War Diary.

APPENDIX 'A'.

MOVEMENTS OF BATTALIONS &c. DURING RELIEF.
****

DATE.	UNIT.	FROM.	TO.	REMARKS.
Feb. 25th.	2/Irish Guards.	BILLON	MAUREPAS	
	3/Coldstream Guards	MAUREPAS	BILLON	
	2nd Gds.Bde.M.G.Co. and T.M.Batt.	BILLON	MAUREPAS.	
Feb. 26th.	2/Coldstream Guards	LINE	MAUREPAS	
	2/Grenadier Guards	MAUREPAS	BILLON	
	2/Irish Guards	MAUREPAS	LINE (Left Sector)	
	2nd Gds.Bde. M.G.Co. and T.M.Batt.	MAUREPAS	LINE.	
	1st Gds.Bde. M.G.Co. and T.M.Batt.	LINE	MAUREPAS	
	3/Grenadier Guards	BILLON	MAUREPAS	
	75th Field Co.R.E. 76th Field Co.R.E. 55th Field Co.R.E.	LINE MAUREPAS BRONFAY.	BRONFAY LINE MAUREPAS	Not to move before noon.
Feb. 27th.	1/Irish Guards	LINE	MAUREPAS	
	1/Scots Guards	PRIEZ	MAUREPAS	
	3/Grenadier Guards	MAUREPAS	LINE (Right Sector)	
	2/Coldstream Guards	MAUREPAS	VILLE	Rail from PLATEAU.
	2/Scots Guards	VILLE	PRIEZ	Rail to PLATEAU.

(Continued).

Sheet 2. (APPENDIX 'A').

DATE.	UNIT.	FROM.	TO.	REMARKS.
Feb. 27th.	1st Guards Bde Hd.Qrs.	LINE.	BILLON.	
	2nd Guards Bde.Hd.Qrs.	BILLON.	LINE.	
	1st Guards Bde. M.G. Co. and T.M.Batt.	MAUREPAS.	BILLON.	
Feb. 28th.	1/Irish Guards.	MAUREPAS.	BILLON.	
	1/Coldstream Guards.	BILLON.	MAUREPAS.	

(*) Times of these moves will be issued by the Division.

Times for all other moves will be arranged between Guards Brigades concerned.

Times for movements of R.E. units will be settled by C.R.E.

APPENDIX 'B'.

DISTRIBUTION OF GUARDS BRIGADES ON COMPLETION OF RELIEF.

BRIGADE IN THE LINE	DIVISIONAL RESERVE	CORPS RESERVE
2nd Guards Brigade.	**1st Guards Brigade.**	**3rd Guards Brigade.**
Brigade Hd.Qrs. - BOIS DOUAGE at b.4.c.3.2.	Brigade Hd.Qrs. - BILLON.	Brigade Hd.Qrs. - VILLE.
2/Irish Guards - LINE (Left).	2/Grenadier Guards - BILLON.	4/Grenadier Guards - VILLE.
3/Grenadier Guards - LINE (Right).	3/Coldstream Guards - BILLON.	1/Grenadier Guards - MERICOURT.
2nd Gds.Bde.M.G. Co. & T.M.Batt. - LINE.	1/Irish Guards - BILLON.	1/Welsh Guards - MERICOURT.
1/Scots Guards - MAUREPAS.	1st Gds.Bde. M.G. Co. & T.M.Batt. - BILLON.	3rd Gds.Bde.M.Co. & T.M.Batt. - TREUX.
1/Coldstream Guards - MAUREPAS	75th Field Co. R.E. - BRONFAY.	-----
2/Scots Guards - PRIEZ FARM	55th Field Co. R.E. - MAUREPAS.	2/Coldstream Guards - VILLE.
76th Field Co. R.E. - LINE.		

SECRET

G.D. No.2709/2/G.

G.D.A.
C.R.E.
1st Guards Brigade.
2nd Guards Brigade.
3rd Guards Brigade.
Pioneer Battalion.
Signals.
A.D.M.S.
"Q".

----

1. Between 2nd and 5th March, the Division will extend its left as far as U.8.B.2.2.

    2nd Guards Brigade will extend its left to approximately U.15.c.0.0. 3rd Guards Brigade will take over thence to U.8.B.2.2.

2. Northern Divisional Boundary on completion of this relief will run as shewn on attached tracing.

    The normal distribution of the Division will then be:-

<u>Guards Brigade in Right Sector.</u>   (Hd.Qrs. BOIS DOUAGE).

2 Battalions	Front System.
1 Battalion	PRIEZ FARM.
1 Battalion	MAUREPAS.

<u>Guards Brigade in Left Sector.</u>   (Hd.Qrs. COMBLES or HAIE WOOD).

2 Battalions	Front System.
1 Battalion	FREGICOURT and HAIE WOOD.
1 Battalion	MAUREPAS.

<u>Guards Brigade in Divisional Reserve.</u>

Brigade Hd.Qrs. & 3 Battalions	BILLON FARM.
1 Battalion	BRONFAY.

    Divisional Hd.Qrs. will remain at MAUREPAS.

3. Detailed orders for the above relief will be issued later.

<u>ACKNOWLEDGE.</u>

C P Heywood

Lieut-Colonel,
General Staff, Guards Divn.

22nd February 1917.

1st Guards Brigade Intelligence Report.
----
8 A.M. Feb: 24th to 8 A.M. Feb: 25th.

OPERATIONS.

   Patrols - No. 5 Post - An Officers patrol and several listening patrols went out from this Post at various intervals during the night. They found the ground between the trenches very much cut up.

   No. 10 Post - Patrol went out from this Post from 3-30 to 4-45 A.M. The enemy were heard working on an old sap at U 26 a 4.5., 60 yards distant and from and opposite No. 10 Post.

   No's. 13, 16 and 22 Posts - Listening patrols remained out from these Posts during most of the night. They saw a small party working on the German wire and heard sounds of baling and working. One patrol heard the sound of Transport from the direction of GOVERNMENT Farm.

   No. 21 Post - An Officers patrol went out from this Post with instructions to reconnoitre the enemy's line at U 20 d 6.7. The enemy's wire was reached at a distance of 150 to 180 yards from our Post. The wire formed a Salient, behind which men were working with picks. They were probably joining up two Posts at U 20 d 4 1/2.7. From the Salient the wire turned back slightly towards the South. It was badly damaged in two or three places. Otherwise it appeared to be fairly strong. The patrol then returned having found that the ground was in good condition and that the walking was easy.

INTELLIGENCE. Continuous smoke was seen issuing from a large heap of chalk at about U 26 a 7 1/2.1 1/2. At about 7-15 A.M. three men dressed in full marching order with packs and steel helmets emerged from this supposed dugout and disappeared into their front line.

   Various other parties were seen from the left Battalion front to be in the vicinity of U 26 c 7.2., U 26 a 7 1/2. 1 1/2., U 26 a 8.2. and U 26 c 8.5.

   The enemy's wire to the South of A P 2 appears to be very weak.

AIRCRAFT. Nil.

ARTILLERY. The activity was much below normal. There was slight retaliation for our wire cutting.

MACHINE GUNS. 1500 rounds of indirect fire were used during the night by the guns in our Reserve line at targets in U 21 d and U 22 c.

DESERTER. Two Germans who approached our line last night were fired upon. One of them returned a second time shouting 'Kamerad'. He was taken in at No. 15 Post.

                                                  Captain,
                            for Brigade Major, 1st Guards Brigade.

SECRET.   (329)   COPY No.

1st Guards Brigade Order No. 102.

Ref. Map - TRENCH MAP 1/10,000.   Feb: 25th, 1917.

1. (a) Information has been received from prisoners that the enemy intend falling back on a line East of CAMBRAI by March 26th.

    (b) All Divisions of the XIV Corps have been ordered to send out strong patrols tonight to ascertain whether the German trenches on their front have been vacated and to gain all possible ground.

2. (a) The Right Battalion (1st Bn. Irish Guards) will reconnoitre their front -

    (i)   From U 26 d 9.8. to U 26 a 9.0.
    (ii) From U 26 a 7.2. to U 26 a 6.8.

    (b) The Left Battalion (2nd Bn. Coldstream Guards) will reconnoitre their front with four separate detachments -

    (i)   U 20 d 9.8. to U 20 d 5.7.
    (ii) U 20 d 5.7. to U 20 d 1½.5.
    (iii) U 20 d 1½.5. to U 20 d 0.2.
    (iv) U 20 d 0.2. to U 16 a 9.8.

3. All patrols will be of fighting strength and will consist of a proportion of Bombers.

4. All patrols will move forward from our lines at 9 P.M. and will work from North to South of the Sectors allotted to them.

5. If gaps are found in the enemy's wire, patrols must try and push through into the enemy's trench with a view to :-

    (i)   Of gaining information.
    (ii) Of capturing a prisoner.
    (iii) Of holding the trench if unoccupied.

6. If patrols report that the enemy have withdrawn from their front line O.C's 2nd Bn. Coldstream Guards and 1st Bn. Irish Guards will be prepared to send forward troops to occupy it. If it is found possible to occupy the enemy's front line, O.C. Battalions will at once push patrols forward again to reconnoitre enemy's support trenches.

7. If troops are pushed forward to occupy old German line an equal number of troops can be moved up from the Reserve line.

8. O.C., 1st Bn. Scots Guards at PRIEZ Farm will be prepared to push forward troops as may be ordered to the Reserve line to take the place of any troops moved forward by O.C., 2nd Bn. Coldstream Guards and O.C., 1st Bn. Irish Guards.

9. The Battalions in Reserve at MAUREPAS will hold themselves in readiness to move if required.

10. O.C's. Right and Left Group, Guards Divnl. Artillery, will arrange to sweep tracks and trenches in U 21 c and d and U 27 a and b. at intervals during the night.

11. O.C., 1st Guards Bde. Machine Gun Company will not bring any fire to bear on enemy's tracks or trenches tonight except in the event of an "S.O.S."

12. Brigade H.Q., will remain at BOIS DOUAGE and must be kept informed of every move.
O.C., 2nd Bn. Coldstream Guards and 1st Bn. Irish Guards will keep each other informed of all movements and also the Battalions on their outer flanks.

ACKNOWLEDGE.

Captain,
Brigade Major, 1st Guards Brigade.

Issued at 5 P.M.

2nd Bn. Grenadier Guards.
2nd Bn. Coldstream Guards.
1st Bn. Irish Guards.
1st Bn. Scots Gds. (PRIEZ Farm).
2nd Bn. Irish Guards (MAUREPAS).

Guards Division.
Right Group, G.D.A.
Left Group, G.D.A.
Right Brigade.
Left Brigade.
75th Field Coy., R.E.

Copy No ..5..

GUARDS DIVISION ORDER NO. 110.

1. On the morning of February 28th, operations are to be carried out as under at a Zero hour which will be notified later.

(a) 29th Division are to capture enemy trenches from U.14.B.8½.1½ to about U.8.D.2½.9½.

(b) 20th Division are to simultaneously advance their line in N.36.C.

2. Guards Divisional Artillery will cooperate as follows:-

(a) Three 18 pdr. batteries will be placed at disposal of 29th Division from 2 hours before Zero to 4 p.m. on 28th February.

(b) Three 18 pdr. batteries other than those mentioned in (a), will barrage enemy front line from U.15.A.30.15 - U.15.C.5.7 - U.15.C.6.0 from Zero to Zero + 90 minutes.

These batteries will be at disposal of Guards Division in case of counter attack on Guards Divisional front.

Details of tasks (a) and (b) have been notified to G.O.C. R.A. by 29th Division and XIV Corps Artillery respectively.

(c) Likely assembly places in U.21.B and D, including RHINE Trench and BEETHOVEN Trench will be shelled at intervals from Zero to Zero + 48 hours.

3. 2nd Guards Brigade will arrange to bring bursts of long range machine gun fire of not less than four machine guns onto RHINE Trench from Zero to Zero + 48 hours.

Arrangements will be made by 2nd Guards Brigade that intelligence of any enemy movement about RHINE Trench is rapidly communicated to machine guns so that advantage may be taken of such targets.

2.

4.   2nd Guards Brigade will, if wind is favourable, discharge smoke on the front U.20.C.5.0 - U.20.B.3.2, discharge to commence at Zero.

Instructions as to this smoke discharge will be issued separately to 2nd Guards Brigade.

G.O.C. 2nd Guards Brigade will be responsible for deciding whether smoke is to be discharged, or not.

5.   Watches will be synchronised at 1 p.m. and 7 p.m. on February 27th.

ACKNOWLEDGE.

CPHeywood

Lieut-Colonel,
23rd February 1917.   General Staff. Guards Divn.

Issued to Divnl. Signals at 4 p.m.

Copy No.			
1	General Staff.	8	Pioneer Battalion.
2	"Q".	9	Signals.
3	G.D.A.	10	A.D.M.S.
4	C.R.E.	11	29th Division.
5	1st Guards Brigade.	12	40th Division.
6	2nd Guards Brigade.	13	XIV Corps.
7	3rd Guards Brigade.	14	War Diary.

****

Copy No ..5..

GUARDS DIVISION ORDER NO. 111.

1. (a) 1st Guards Brigade will carry out a raid tomorrow night (February 26th/27th) with the object of finding out in what strength the enemy is holding his trenches.

(b) In the event of the enemy being found in small numbers, 1st Guards Brigade will be prepared to push forward troops to support the raiding party and extend their hold on enemy's front line.

In the event of more than 200 yards of enemy trench being captured in this manner, such gains will be held.

If less than 200 yards of enemy trench are captured, the decision as to whether the captured portion of the trench is to be held or not will be left to G.O.C. 1st Guards Brigade.

(c) Subsequent to any considerable gain in enemy's front line trench, strong patrols will be pushed forward to ascertain if his support line is held.

2. Arrangements for Artillery support, and wire-cutting, will be made direct between G.O.C. R.A. and G.O.C. 1st Guards Brigade.

A C K N O W L E D G E .

CP Heywood
Lieut-Colonel,
General Staff, Guards Divn.

25th February 1917.

Issued to Divnl. Signals at 9 p.m.

Copy No. 1 General Staff.   8 A.D.M.S.
         2 "Q".   9 Signals.
         3 G.D.A.   10 Pioneer Battalion.
         4 C.R.E.   11 29th Division.
         5 1st Guards Brigade. 12 40th Division.
         6 2nd Guards Brigade. 13 XIV Corps.
         7 3rd Guards Brigade. 14 War Diary.

ORDERS

1st G.B. No.1766.

3rd Bn. Grenadier Guards.	Guards Division.
2nd Bn. Coldstream Guards.	2nd Guards Brigade.
1st Bn. Irish Guards.	Right Group, G.D.A.
2nd Bn. Irish Guards.	Left Group, G.D.A.
1st Gds.Bde.M.G.Company.	Right Brigade.
1st Gds.Bde.T.M.Battery.	Left Brigade.

1. Reference the Brigadiers conversation with O.C's, 2nd Bn. Coldstream Guards and 1st Bn. Irish Guards this morning, no operation will be carried out to-night.

2. Right and Left Group, Guards Divnl. Artillery, will cut wire during to-day at the following places :-

   U.20.d.1½.5. (complete existing gap).
   U.26.a.6.4.

3. Patrols will be sent out by O.C., 1st Bn. Irish Guards and O.C., 2nd Bn. Irish Guards to-night to reconnoitre and report on the effitiveness of the Artillery wire-cutting.

4. (a) On relief to-night, O.C., 2nd Bn. Coldstream Guards will arrange to leave behind guides from the patrol which went out last night from No. 16 Post and reported enemy wire damaged by our Artillery fire about U.20.d.1½.5. (opposite No. 15 Post).

   (b) Similarly to-morrow night O.C., 1st Bn. Irish Guards will arrange to leave a guide behind from the patrol which he will send out to-night to reconnoitre any wire cutting that may be done by Guards Divnl. Artillery to-day at U.26.a.6.4.

5. O.C., 3rd Bn. Grenadier Guards will arrange to send up an Officer to report at H.Q., 1st Bn. Irish Guards, to-morrow morning.
   This Officer will be shown in daylight the point at which any wire has been cut.

6. Units are reminded that if gaps in the German wire are made, they must be kept open at night by Lewis Gun fire before and after patrols go out.
   Lewis Guns should be laid on the gaps by day.
   The gap on the Right Battalion front should be covered from the direction of No. 4 Post.

ACKNOWLEDGE.

26th February 1917.

Captain,
Brigade Major, 1st Guards Brigade.

FINAL NOTES ON THE LINE.

Front line posts are on the whole good. A little progress has been made towards joining up No's 3 to 10 by utilising the old derelict trench. It is possible to get along this trench, but it will require deepening, revetting, and boarding before it is of much use.

Front line wire is fairly strong in front of right Battalion, but less strong in front of left Battalion. It is being continued between No's 2 and 3 posts (in rear of the Advanced Posts), so as to make a continuous line in case these should go. A switch has been carried back along the line of the Right Divisional boundary from No.1 Post to RANCOURT, in order to protect our right flank.

Support line. In right Sector No's 1, 2, 3 posts are in fairly good order and progress has been made towards digging a line between these and across the gap between No.3 Post and No.6 Post (right post of left sector).
In left sector less progress has been made with support line, but posts 6 and 7, 9 and 10, (which were in very bad order) have been considerably improved.
In the gap progress has been made with deep dug-outs on the sites of No's 4 and 5 posts (projected). A Vickers gun has been placed in BISHOPS AVENUE at a point where there is an old dug-out (about U 25 b 9.6.) in order to block the gap.
Work on a deep dug-out for right front Company H.Q., in No.3 Support Post has been just begun.
It is a question whether it would not be a good thing to move No's 9 and 10 Support Posts. Both are in full view of the enemy from the right front and are apt to be badly shelled. Neither is a good post.

Support line wire. The support line is now wired throughout it's length. The wire is strong and good in front of most of right sector, but wants strengthening in front of left sector and across gap. It has been extended to our right to join up with support line wire of XV Corps in front of RANCOURT.

Communications.
A new duck-board track has been laid from Right Duckboards at about U 25 d 6.8. to No.1 Support post, making a new and shorter route up to the right front and Support posts.
Two new communication trenches have been dug up to No.7A. Post from about U 26 a 1½.2. and U 26 a 0.3½. respectively. These are deep and good and the revetting and boarding is nearly complete. They afford covered access by day to 7A Post. It would be a good thing if these were camouflaged, at least in parts. It is proposed to firestep these for fire outwards, so as to form a supporting point.
Other communication trenches have been begun, but not much progress has been made with them. One in left sector from Orchard via Observation Post to front line is nearly through to Observation Post, but is not revetted.

Strong Points.
Cruciform requires much revetting and fire positions extending. At present there are not enough fire positions for the garrison. It also requires wiring. The dug-out is now complete and the Post has been recently occupied by 2 Sections and a Machine Gun.
A Post has been dug, (but not revetted) at about U 26 c 7.3. to protect our right flank in case of a break-through in front of RANCOURT. This wants a good deal of work to finish it, but should be a useful post.
Another flanking post is projected about U 26 c 2.3., but this has not been commenced.

Instructions No. 1 for FREGICOURT Sector.

1. Roster of reliefs.

Date.	Front Line.		Reserve in MAUREPAS.	
	Left Bn.	Right Bn.	Left.	Right.
Feb: 19th.	3/C.G.	1/I.G. out.	2/C.G.	3/G.G. out.
		2/G.G. in.		1/I.G. in.
20th.	3/C.G.	2/G.G.	2/C.G.	1/I.G.
21st.	3/C.G.	2/G.G.	2/C.G.	1/I.G.
22nd.	3/C.G. out.	2/G.G.	2/C.G. out.	1/I.G.
	2/C.G. in.		3/C.G. in.	
23rd.	2/C.G.	2/G.G. out.	3/C.G.	1/I.G. out.
		1/I.G. in.		3/G.G. in.
24th.	2/C.G.	1/I.G.	3/C.G.	3/G.G.
25th.	2/C.G.	1/I.G.	3/C.G.	3/G.G.
26th.	2/C.G. out.	1/I.G.	–	–
27th.	–	1/I.G. out.	–	–

2. Arrangements for relief will be made direct between Units concerned.

S E C R E T.   1st G.B. No. 1509.

2nd Bn. Grenadier Guards.   50th Infantry Brigade.
2nd Bn. Coldstream Guards.   119th Infantry Brigade.
3rd Bn. Coldstream Guards.   Right Group) G.D.A.
1st Bn. Irish Guards.   Left Group)
Bde. Machine Gun Company.   75th Field Coy., R.E.
1st Guards T.M. Battery.   Town Major, MAUREPAS.
Guards Division.   Staff Captain.
1st Gds. Bde. Supply Officer.   O.C., Signals.
1st Gds. Bde. Transport Officer.

---

1. Herewith amended Page 1 for Instructions No. 1 which were sent you on Feb: 8th.

2. Please acknowledge receipt.

                                                M B Smith
                                                Captain,
19th Feb: 1917.   Brigade Major, 1st Guards Brigade.

SECRET.   1st Guards Bde. No. 1509.

2nd Bn. Grenadier Guards.   25th Infantry Brigade.
2nd Bn. Coldstream Guards.   52nd Infantry Brigade.
3rd Bn. Coldstream Guards.   Right Group) G.D.A.
1st Bn. Irish Guards.   Left Group)
Bde. Machine Gun Company.   75th Field Coy., R.E.
1st Guards T. M. Battery.   Town Major, MAUREPAS.
Guards Division.   Staff Captain.
1st Gds. Bde. Supply Officer.   O.C., Signals.
1st Gds. Bde. Transport Officer.

Instructions No. 1 for FREGICOURT Sector.

1.   Roster of reliefs.

Date.	Front Line.		Reserve in MAUREPAS.	
	Left Bn.	Right Bn.	Left.	Right.
Feb: 10th	2/S.G. out. 3/C.G. in.	1/G.G.	3/C.G. out. 2/S.G. in.	2/G.G. in.
11th	3/C.G.	1/G.G. out. 2/G.G. in.	2/S.G. out. 3/C.G. in.	2/G.G. out. 1/G.G. in.
12th	3/C.G.	2/G.G.	3/C.G.	1/G.G. out. 1/I.G. in.
13th	3/C.G.	2/G.G.	3/C.G.	1/I.G.
14th	3/C.G. out. 2/C.G. in.	2/G.G.	2/C.G. out. 3/C.G. in.	1/I.G.
15th	2/C.G.	2/G.G. out. 1/I.G. in.	3/C.G.	1/I.G. out. 2/G.G. in.
16th	2/C.G.	1/I.G.	3/C.G.	2/G.G.
17th	2/C.G.	1/I.G.	3/C.G.	2/G.G.
18th	2/C.G. out. 3/C.G. in.	1/I.G.	3/C.G. out. 2/C.G. in.	2/G.G.

2.   Arrangements for relief will be made direct between Units concerned.

(2)

3. The hour of reliefs must be changed from time to time.

4. Units moving into the line will send on an advanced party of not less than 1 N.C.O. per Company and per Battn., H.Q.,

Units moving into the Camps will send on a party to take over Camps and any work in hand.

5. All movement East of M'URBEAS must be by Platoons in file at 200 yards interval.

6. Completion of all movements will be reported to Brigade Headquarters.

7. The instructions laid down in G.D. 252/8/A of Jan: 13th will be carried out by Units the day on which Units move into the line and the day after they come out. Units will give the N.C.O. in charge of the special bath at M'URBF'S notice of when they intend to use the bath and will provide him with fuel and ingredients for the soap.

8. The Soup Kitchen is situated at PRIEZ Farm.

ACKNOWLEDGE.

Captain,

8th February 1917.   Brigade Major, 1st Guards Brigade.

S E C R E T.

2nd Bn. Grenadier Gds.
2nd Bn. Coldstream Gds.
3rd Bn. Coldstream Gds.
1st Bn. Irish Gds.
1st Guards M.G. Coy.
1st Guards T.M. Battery.

1st Guards Bde. No. 1509/1/1.

Instructions No. 2 for PUISIEUX Sector.

SUBJECT - Work.

1. Until further orders the following work will be carried out in the Brigade Sector:-

   (a) By Battalions in the Line.
      (i) Construction of three communication trenches to the front line posts in each Battalion Sector.
      (ii) Connecting up front line posts.
   (b) By 75th Coy. R.E. (With working party from Battalions).
      (i) Construction of Support Line.
      (ii) Wiring of Support Line.
      (iii) Construction of Company H.Q. for Right Reserve Company of Right Battalion.
      (iv) Construction of dugouts for M.G. Company.

2. Sapping platoons will go in and out of the trenches with their Battalions.
   They will be employed under the O.C. Battalions on the C.T.'s mentioned in para. 1 (a), and not on the Support Line as detailed in Brigade Orders of today. They may also be employed on revetting trenches which may be dug to laterally connect front line posts.

3. For the purpose of carrying out the work mentioned in para. 1 (b) the following proceedure will be adopted:-
   (a) Each Battalion in the line will detail daily 1 Officer and 100 men from the Reserve Companies with tools, for digging the new Support Line.
      An Officer of 75th Field Coy. will report at Right and Left Battalion H.Q. every morning at 8 a.m. starting tomorrow, Feb. 18th, to point out the work to be done to the Officer who will be in charge of the party carrying it out.
      Arrangements will then be made with the R.E. Officer concerned as to what hour the work will start that day or evening.
      On relief days the outgoing Battalion will find this party.
   (b) Each Battalion in the line will detail 1 N.C.O. and 15 men for wiring the Support Line. This party to report to a representative of 75th Field Coy. at Battalion H.Q. at 5.50 p.m. daily. This party to be found by outgoing Battalion on relief nights. *starting tomorrow Feb 18th*

4. R.E. Dumps are situated at:-

   G 1 a 4.2 for Right Battalion.
   U 19 a 6.2 for Left Battalion.

   These Dumps are under 75th Coy. R.E., and Units will wire direct to 75th Coy. R.E. by 8 p.m. daily what they intend to draw the following day.

17th February 1917.

Captain,
Brigade Major, 1st Guards Brigade.

SECRET.

1st Guards Bde. No. 1509/2

2nd Bn. Grenadier Gds.
2nd Bn. Coldstream Gds.
3rd Bn. Coldstream Gds.
1st Bn. Irish Gds.
1st Guards M.G.Coy.
1st Guards T.M.Battery.

INSTRUCTIONS NO. 3 FOR FREGICOURT SECTOR.

Subject - RETURNS.

1. The following Returns will be rendered daily by the two Battalions in the front line :-

	Due Brigade H.Q.
Morning report (by wire)	3.30 a.m.
Intelligence Report by orderly	10.0 a.m.
Evening report (by wire)	3.30 p.m.
Casualty report (by wire, in code, covering period 12 noon to 12 noon).	3.30 p.m.
Demand for R.E.Stores, etc., direct to 75th Field Coy. R.E.	8.0 p.m.

2. The Machine Gun Company in the line will render an Intelligence report to reach these H.Q., at 10 a.m. daily, also a Casualty report - Nil returns to be rendered.

3. Battalions in the Camps and the Trench Mortar Battery will only render Casualty returns if they have casualties to report.

4. The Intelligence report should be rendered under the following headings :-

   1. Operations - (Patrols and Sniping).
   2. Intelligence.
   3. Aircraft.
   4. Artillery.
   5. Work - Number of coils of wire put out to be stated.

   Map references should be given if possible. Approximate Map references are of great assistance but if they are only approximate, this fact should be stated.

   This report will cover the period from 8.30 a.m. to 8.30 a.m.

5. An outgoing Battalion must be careful to hand over the d days' Intelligence to the incoming Battalion.

6. Situation reports do not always show the true situation on the Battalion front and an effort should be made to make them of some real value as a Situation report.

7. The capture of a prisoner must be wired at once to Bde. H.Q., the Regiment to which the prisoner belongs being stated.

ACKNOWLEDGE.

9th February 1917.

Captain,
Brigade Major, 1st Guards Brigade.

SECRET.   1st Guards Bde. No. 1548.

2nd Bn. Grenadier Gds.
2nd Bn. Coldstream Gds.
3rd Bn. Coldstream Gds.
1st Bn. Irish Gds.
1st Guards M.G. Coy.
1st Guards T.M. Battery.

1.   The Corps Commander has laid down that the policy to be followed on the Divisional Front for the present is to be strictly defensive.

        As has been laid down in Instructions No. 2, the first necessity is to make a continuous Support Line, and to push forward thence communications to front line posts.

        Until this work is completed, and reliefs can be carried out below ground, instead of in full view of the enemy as is at present the case, the action of snipers, Stokes mortar batteries and machine guns will not be such as to stir up the enemy or cause him to delay our work and harass our reliefs.

2.   Attention is drawn to the first portion of para. (e) of the Principles of Defence laid down in Appendix "A" of the Defence Scheme.

        All Commanders should understand that if the enemy succeeds in establishing himself in any part of our front line he must be <u>immediately</u> counter attacked from both flanks and from the support line where this exists and is sufficiently close to the front line.

3.   Nothing in this order is to be taken as the smallest excuse for any kind of fraternising or friendly relations with the enemy, nor for any of our men exposing themselves unnecessarily.

                                                        Captain,
10th February 1917.   Brigade Major, 1st Guards Bde.

SECRET.

2nd Bn. Grenadier Gds.
2nd Bn. Coldstream Gds.
3rd Bn. Coldstream Gds.
1st Bn. Irish Gds.

1st Guards Bde. No. 1509/3.

INSTRUCTIONS NO. 4 for FREGICOURT SECTOR.

SUBJECT - Artillery.

1. The front of the Brigade is covered by Guards Divisional Artillery subdivided into two groups.
   Right Group (H.Q. B.11.a.4.7.) covers the Right Battalion front, and is under command of Lt.Col. A.B.BETHELL, D.S.O.
   Left Group (H.Q. T.28.a.9.0.) covers the Left Battalion front, and is under the command of Lt.Col. F.A.BUZZARD, D.S.O.

2. Battalions H.Q. are in direct communication with their Group H.Q., and with the batteries in their group.

3. A liaison Officer remains at Battalion H.Q. by night, and at the O.P. by day.

4. Frequent "tests" are to be carried out from the front line, in calling for artillery fire.

5. The proceedure will be:-
   Infantry will send down
   (a) "Test" followed by number of a trench, e.g. "Test U.26/7",
   or (b) "Test" followed by Right or Left Group e.g. "Test Right Group",
   or (c) "Test".
   In the case of (a) the 18 pdr. battery which covers this trench will fire opposite the trench named.
   In the case of (b) all the 18 pdr. batteries of the Group named will fire on their S.O.S. lines.
   In the case of (c) all the 18 pdr. batteries of the Divisional Artillery will fire on their S.O.S. lines.

6. In all cases, by day one round per gun will be fired; by night, one round per battery.

7. (a) will be called for by Company Commanders.
   (b) will be called for by Battalion Commanders.
   (c) will be called for by Guards Bde. H.Q.

8. "Tests carried out will be reported in the morning or evening reports of the Guards Brigade in the line. The times of despatch of the test message and of the opening of fire by the guns concerned will be stated.

9. Company Commanders will call for a test in front of certain trenches once during their Company tour in the front line, the result being reported as directed in para. 8.

10. Commanding Officers are reminded of the Major-General's wishes that the relations of Guards Officers with Artillery Officers should be of the most friendly description. The Brigadier hopes that all Officers will do all in their power to this end.

ACKNOWLEDGE.

12th February 1917.

Captain,
Brigade Major, 1st Guards Bde.

SECRET.   1st G.B. No.1509/4.

2nd Bn. Grenadier Guards.
2nd Bn. Coldstream Guards.
3rd Bn. Coldstream Guards.
1st Bn. Irish Guards.

Instructions No. 5 for FREGICOURT Sector.

Subject :- MISCELLANEOUS.

1. **WOOD FOR FUEL.**

    During the present cold weather every man going into the trenches will carry up a small bundle of wood for burning purposes, when in the trenches.

    This wood will be collected under Battn., arrangements while Battn's. are in the Camps at MAUREPAS, and issued to the troops before they go into the trenches.

    Any timber can be cut in the BOIS DOUAGE - MAUREPAS - BOIS FAVIERE, but drift wood lying on the ground must be taken before any standing timber is cut down.

    Battn's. cutting wood in the BOIS DOUAGE may make a Dump at Brigade H.Q., This dump will be guarded for the Battn. to which it belongs by Brigade H.Q.,

    If the above is carried out there should be no excuse for any cutting of revetting material for fire wood

2. **TRAINING.**

    Battn's. in the Camps at MAUREPAS are not expected to do any training on the first day after they come out of the trenches beyond inspection of rifles - respirators - equipment, etc. but on the second and third days some drill and training must be carried out. The training of the Lewis Gunners and Bombers must not be lost sight of.

    There is a Brigade Store of bombs, ammunition, etc. in the Camp at MAUREPAS and Units can draw from this Store if an indent is sent to Brigade H.Q., a few hours in advance.

3. **PATROLLING.**

    Patrols should be sent out under systematic arrangements every night and should always be given some definite objective.

    No opportunity must be missed of surprising an enemy patrol and Units are again reminded of the advantage of a rifle over a bomb for this kind of work.

    The O.C., Right Front Battn., will arrange to reconnoitre and report on the enemy wire from U 26 a 6.6 to U 26 a 7.0. Enemy saps and listening posts in front of both Battn., Sectors must be reconnoitred and reported on, as soon as possible.

4. **OBSERVATION.**

    Systematic observation of the enemy lines must be started as soon as possible.

14th February 1917.   Captain,
                                            Brigade Major, 1st Guards Brigade.

SECRET.   1st Guards Bde. No. 1509/5.

    2nd Bn. Grenadier Gds.
    2nd Bn. Coldstream Gds.
    3rd Bn. Coldstream Gds.
    1st Bn. Irish Gds.
    1st Guards M.G. Coy.
    1st Guards T.M. Battery.

Instructions No. 6 for FREGICOURT Sector.

SUBJECT:- Defensive Policy.

1. The Defensive Policy laid down by the Corps Commander to be adopted on this Brigade front, does not mean that the enemy is to be allowed to walk about in broad daylight in the vicinity of his front line.

2. The practice of allowing the enemy to do this without being shot at must cease at once, and any German attempting to show himself must be fired upon.

3. Any of our men who expose themselves needlessly, or walk across the open in daylight will have their names taken, and will be severely dealt with.

4. The only point at which any kind of live and let live policy may be adopted is opposite Nos. 1, 2 and 3 Advanced Posts on the right of the Right Battalion front, but even here men of either side must not be allowed to walk about in the open in daylight.

5. If any men - as for instance, guides - have to be withdrawn from posts which cannot be reached except by going across the open, they must be withdrawn before daylight.

6. At present anyone who wishes to get to any part of the Right Battalion front in daylight, passes by No. 7a Post. Only those who wish to get to Nos. 6, 7 or 8 Posts must be allowed to pass by No. 7a Post, and then all ranks must be made to keep to the old C.T. until out of sight over the crest.

7. In order to facilitate communication with the posts to the South of No. 6 Post, the O.C. Right Battalion will at once arrange to lay the new duckboard track which branches off from the present right hand duckboards at about U 25 d 6.7, for which duckboards have been carried up but not yet put properly in position.

                                                              Captain,

19th February 1917.   Brigade Major, 1st Guards Bde.

S E C R E T.   33 4/2   1st G.B. No. 1525/2.

Amendment to 1st Guards Brigade Defence Scheme.

1. Para. 1.   Northern Boundary of Divnl. Area.   Line 5.
   for B 7 a 4.8. read B 7 c 4.8.

2. Add at end of Appendix "B.1." -

   NOTE - In the event of an attack 2 Guns from the Brigade
   Reserve will move without awaiting Orders to the
   Intermediate Line and occupy positions at -

   T 30 d 1.85.   (M.2.)
   T 30 a 9.2.   (M.3.)

18th Feb: 1917.

Captain,
Brigade Major, 1st Guards Brigade.

SECRET.   1st G.B. No.1325/1.

2nd Bn. Grenadier Gds..   50th Infantry Brigade.
2nd Bn. Coldstream Gds..   119th Infantry Brigade.
3rd Bn. Coldstream Gds..   Right Group, G.D.A.
1st Bn. Irish Gds..   Left Group; G.D.A.
1st Guards M.G.Company.   75th Field Coy., R.E.
1st Guards T.M.Battery.   O.C., PRIEZ FARM Battalion.
Guards Division.

1. Herewith 1st Guards Brigade Defence Scheme for the FRESNICOURT Sector.

2. Appendices B.1. and E are attached. Appendices B.2. and C and D will be detached from 1st Guards Brigade Provisional Defence Scheme now in your possession.

3. 1st Guards Brigade Provisional Defence Scheme will be destroyed with exception of Appendices B.2. C. and D.

4. Appendix A, Principles of Defence, has been issued to Units concerned.

5. ACKNOWLEDGE.

17th February 1917.   Brigade Major, 1st Guards Brigade.
                                                        Captain,

S E C R E T.   Copy No.

1ST GUARDS BRIGADE DEFENCE SCHEME.

Reference Maps - COMBLES 1/10,000.
              BOUCHAVESNES 1/10,000.

1. **BOUNDARIES.**

   The front allotted to Guards Division extends from U 26 c 7.3 to U 20 b 3.2.
   The whole of this front is held by 1st Guards Brigade. The 119th Brigade of 40th Division is on our Right, and Right Group of 17th Division on our Left.

   Southern Boundary of Divisional Area.

   U 26 c 7.3 - U 25 c 25.25 - B 6 c 7.2 - B 5 d 5.1 -

   B 11 c 0.6 - B 10 d 0.2 - (LE FOREST to XV Corps) -

   B 10 c 0.1 - B 9 d 0.0 - B 14 b 5.0 (MAUREPAS to XIV

   Corps) - B 14 a 7.0 - B 14 c 3.7 - B 14 c 0.0 -

   B 19 a 0.4 - A 24 a 6.2 - A 24 a 0.3 - thence along

   North side of PERONNE ROAD to A 22 b 50.25 - across road

   to A 22 b 4.1 - A 22 a 7.2 - A 26 c 6.9.

   Northern Boundary of Divisional Area.

   U 20 b 3.2 - U 20 a 0.7 - U 19 b 8.7 - T 30 a 8.7 -

   T 30 a 0.4 - T 29 b 0.2 - T 28 b 5.2 - thence along

   railway running through COMBLES and along Valley on

   North side of SAVERNAKE ROAD and OAKHANGER WOODS to

   B 8 a 75.80 - B 7 Central - junction of roads B 7 c 4.8 -

   junction of roads A 12 b 9.3 - thence along Western

   outskirts of HARDECOURT to A 12 c 8.0 - FORKED ROADS

   A 18 a 05.90 - A 16 b 8.7.

   INTER-Battalion Boundary. U 26 a 4.8 - U 26 a 0.9 - U 19 d 2.2.

2. **ORGANISATION OF DEFENCE.**

   The defensive system is organised as follows :-

   A. Front Line.   - Consisting of 25 Island Posts.

(2)

B. SUPPORT LINE.
Consisting of 8 Island Posts from 100 to 200 yards in rear of Front line with a strong point on the left flank and a contemplated one on the right flank. The Posts will be joined into a continuous line as soon as the ground permits.

There is a large gap in the centre, between No. 3 and No. 6 Support Posts - No. 4 and No. 5 posts at present not being garrisoned. This gap has been wired throughout, and a Machine Gun is in position at U 25 b 9.6 to cover the gap.

C. RESERVE LINE. - Consisting of 100 yards of BLAMONT RESERVE in the Right Sector, and 200 yards of BLAMONT RESERVE in the Left Sector, connected and supported by 14 Island Posts - from 500 to 800 yards in rear of Support Line.

The following are projected :-

D. INTERMEDIATE LINE. - Already wired throughout and traced out, but not dug - from 800 to 1,200 yards in rear of the Reserve Line.

E. SECOND LINE. - Not yet traced.

3. TACTICAL FEATURES.

The most important tactical feature in the Divisional Area is the ridge which runs from RANCOURT to SAILLY-SAILLISEL.
It is just on the forward slope of this ridge that our Front Line is situated and it is of the utmost importance that the enemy should not gain possession of the ridge.
At present the enemy can only observe the high ground in neighbourhood of intermediate line from the North about. LE TRANSLOY and from the S.E.
It is essential therefore to deny the enemy the observation of the FREGICOURT and LE FOREST VALLEYS, which he would gain by the capture of the RANCOURT - SAILLY-SAILLISEL RIDGE.

4. DISTRIBUTION OF INFANTRY.

A. The Brigade is disposed as follows:-

Brigade Headquarters - BOIS DE DOUAGE - B 4 c 4.2.

Right Front Battalion - H.Q. - B 6 b 5.9.
    1 Coy - Front Line Posts.
    1 Coy - Support Line Posts.
    2 Coys - Reserve Line.

Left Front Battalion - H.Q. - U 27 d 4.8.
    1 Coy - Front Line Posts.
    1 Coy - Support Line Posts.
    2 Coys - Reserve Line.

Brigade Reserve - 2 Battalions - Camps, MAUREPAS.
Brigade M.G. Coy. H.Q. - T 30 b 8.7. For positions of Machine Guns see Appendix.
Brigade T.M.Battery H.Q. - B 6 c 0.8. For positions of Mortars see Appendix.
75th Coy. R.E. - T 29 c 5.5.

(3)

B. The Battalion of the Guards Brigade in Divisional Reserve PRIEZ FARM is also for tactical purposes under the orders of G.O.C., 1st Guards Brigade.

5. ARTILLERY.

The Brigade Front is supported by Guards Divnl. Artillery, divided into Right and Left Groups. One of these Groups is told off for each Battalion Front :-

RIGHT GROUP - H.Q., ARDERLU WOOD - B 11 a 4.7.

LEFT GROUP - H.Q., T 28 a 9.6.

6. ACTION IN THE EVENT OF ATTACK.

(a) In the event of the enemy gaining a footing in any part of our line the troops on both flanks will hold their ground and will on no account give way. Lewis Gun and Rifle Grenade fire will immediately be brought to bear from the flanks on that portion of the line occupied by the enemy. Should this fail to turn the enemy out an immediate counter attack from the Support line posts will be delivered under cover of Rifle Grenade and Lewis Gun barrage.

Each Battalion in the line may draw to the extent of two Platoons from its Reserve line for the purpose of reinforcing its Support line with a view to such counter attacks - but the remainder of the garrison of the Reserve line will hold its ground at all costs.

In the event of the immediate counter attack failing, a counter attack will be organised under Brigade arrangements on the lines indicated in para. 3.

(b) The Commanding Officer and Company Commanders of Battn's. coming into Reserve at PRIEZ FARM must at once reconnoitre the ground and best cross country tracks between PRIEZ FARM and the Reserve line.

(c) Battalions in Reserve at MAUREPAS must be prepared to move on receipt of Orders and Commanding Officers and Company Commdrs. must reconnoitre the ground and best cross country tracks to PRIEZ FARM as soon as possible after arrival in the Camps at MAUREPAS.

On receipt of the message "Defence Scheme Prepare to move", C.O's of these Battn's. will report at Brigade H.Q., as soon as possible.

These Battn's. will draw 2 bombs, an extra bandolier of S.A.A. and 2 sandbags per man and 50 flares per Battn., from the Brigade Store in MAUREPAS, as soon as possible after receipt of above message. Troops will parade in fighting order: water-bottles will be filled and if possible one days ration in addition to the iron ration will be carried.

(d) The Reserve Section of Bde. Machine Gun Company will move without awaiting Orders, to the old German gun pits at U 25 a 2.7.

(e) The two Reserve Sections of the Trench Mortar Battery will be prepared to move as ordered.
All Officers of the Battery will reconnoitre the Reserve line and the best means of approach to it.

(f) The Field Coy., R.E. will "Stand To"! in Billets and await Orders.

(g) All fatigue and other parties will report at once to the nearest H.Q.,

7. **GAS.** In the event of Gas Attack, Gas Alert or Gas Shell Bombardment, Units will act upon Fourth Army Standing Orders – "Defence against Gas".

8. The following plan for a counter attack on the SAILLY - RANCOURT Ridge from the Reserve line is issued as a guide to Commdg., Officers and Company Commanders in thinking out their own plans :-

    (a) There will be a heavy preparatory bombardment on that part of the line which has been lost.

    (b) Preliminary Movement: By Zero the assaulting Battn's. or Coy's. from Brigade Reserves will have moved, under cover of darkness, to assembly positions immediately in front of (East of) and close to the wire protecting the Reserve line.

    (c) At Zero the Creeping Barrage will remain stationary for 1 minute, 200 yards in front of Reserve line and will then advance :

    Zero plus 1 minute - 25 yards.
    Zero plus 2 minutes - 50 yards.

    and continue to advance at the rate of 50 yards per minute, to the line of our present "S.O.S" Barrage, where it will remain stationary.
    The stationary barrage on the line referred to in (a) above, will be lifted when the Creeping Barrage reaches it.

    (d) Orders for the lighting of flares by the assaulting troops will be notified at the same time that the Zero hour is notified to Battalions.

    (e) A supply of flares to be kept in the Reserve line, PRIEZ FARM, and MAUREPAS CAMPS for this purpose.

    (f) If a Contac' Aeroplane appears, flares will be lit by our troops still occupying positions in the Front and Support lines after a successful enemy attack, in order to locate the exact area held by the enemy.
    A supply of flares will be kept in the Front and Support lines for this purpose.

MB Smith
Captain,
Brigade Major, 1st Guards Brigade.

APPENDIX "B.1".

DISPOSITION OF MACHINE GUNS.

1. **FRONT LINE SYSTEM** - 6 guns.

H.2.	U 26 a 3.3.	1 gun firing S.E.
H.3.	U 26 a 35.60.	" E. and S.E.
J.1.	U 20 c 4.3.	" N.E.
J.2.	U 20 b 0.2.	" N.E. (enfilading support line wire).
J.3.(CRUCIFORM.) (Strong Point)	U 20 a 3.5.	" N. and N.E.
J.4.	U 25 b 9.6½.	" E. N.E. and S.E.

2. **RESERVE LINE SYSTEM** - 5 guns.

K.1.	U 25 d 0.2.	1 gun firing E. and S.E.
K.2. K.3.	U 25 b 2.7.	2 guns firing N.E. and S.E.
K.4.	U 19 d 2.0.	1 gun firing E. and S.E.
L.1.	U 19 d 4.7.	1 gun firing S.E.

3. **BRIGADE RESERVE** - 5 guns.

    Gorman Gun Pits - U 25 a 0.5. 2 guns.
    FREGICOURT - T 30 a 9.6. 3 guns.

APPENDIX "B.2."

DISPOSITION OF STOKES GUNS.

1 Gun - (offensive, with dug-out) - U.26.a.2.1.
1 Gun - (defensive)   - U.23.a.2.4.
1 Gun - (defensive)   - U.20.c.4.2.
5 Guns- Brigade Reserve.   - PRIEZ FARM.

APPENDIX "C."

MEDICAL ARRANGEMENTS.

Wounded will be carried by hand or rail to Bearer Posts at RANCOURT (O.1.a.3.2.) and PRIEZ FARM (S.6.a.3.5.) for the Right Battalion in the line, and at the FREGICOURT - SAILLISEL SAI ROAD (T.24.b.6.0.) and FREGICOURT (T.30.a.4.7.) for the Left Battalion in the line. From PRIEZ FARM and FREGICOURT Bearer Posts, wounded and sick will be evacuated by motor ambulances to A.D.S. at CG BL C (T.23.d.3.2.) and thence to TRONES WOOD A.D.S. (T.30.a.7.5.), from which they will be evacuated to XIV Corps Main Dressing Station or Rest Station respectively by M.A.C.

APPENDIX "D".

The S.O.S. telephone message or rocket means that the enemy are actually leaving their trenches to attack, and that rapid barrage is required from the Artillery and from Machine Guns that can barrage our front line.

The S.O.S. signal rocket for XIV Corps is one green, one white, one green rocket fired in quick succession and repeated until acted upon by the Artillery.

The S.O.S. signal rockets for XV Corps is a single red and white rocket repeated at intervals until acted on.

==*=*=*=*=*=*=*=*=*=*=*

APPENDIX "E".

Position of Brigade Bomb and S.A.A. Stores.

ADELPHI Dump. (For Right Battn.)	B 6 b 5. 2.
CHARING CROSS Dump. (For Left Battn.)	U 19 a 1.3.
MAUREPAS Dump. (For Reserve Battn.)	Near Town Major's Office, MAUREPAS.
PRIEZ FARM Dump.*(For PRIEZ FARM Battn.)	At Battn. H.Q. PRIEZ FARM.

                10 boxes S.A.A.)
*(A minimum of 100 boxes Mills' bombs) to be left by Battn. in
               1 box flares.)   this Dump).

Position of R.E. and Salvage Dumps.

BARBICAN Dump. (For Right Battn.)	C 1 a 2.1.
BILLINGSGATE Dump. (For Left Battn.)	U 19 a 1.3.

APPENDIX "A".

PRINCIPLES OF DEFENCE.

The following principles will be adopted in holding the line :-

(a) The front line will be held as thinly as is consistent with security. To permit of thus holding the front line, good wire entanglements are necessary, good arrangements for flank defence, and close and continuous observation on the part of Artillery F.O.C's.

(b) Troops will NOT fall back from one line to any other line, but all ground will be defended as long as possible whether the flanks are turned or not.

(c) There are three kinds of attack which may be anticipated:-

(i) A raid.

(ii) An attack on a minor scale to capture some locality, accompanied by a bombardment.

(iii) A serious attack preceded by a heavy bombardment.

(d) <u>As regards (c) (i)</u> :-

Vigilance, active patrolling, combined with a good system of listening posts and wire, make the failure of such attacks certain.

(e) <u>As regards (c) (ii)</u> :-

Should the enemy succeed in establishing himself in our trenches, he should be counter attacked immediately from both flanks and from the support trenches above provided in sufficiently close proximity.

The extent and intensity of the enemy's bombardment if closely observed should give an indication of his objective and enable preparations for counter attack to be made before his attack is delivered. The essential is to deny him time in which to consolidate.

Should the counter attack fail, the captured portion of our trenches must be isolated by blocking, and support trenches firmly held until more deliberate preparations can be made.

Meanwhile, the Artillery will prevent German reinforcements crossing "No Man's Land", and the Infantry must do their utmost to reconnoitre and locate the exact position held by the enemy, so that our Artillery may bombard the captured trenches with precision: thus further counter attack by our reserves will be executed under the most favourable conditions.

Artillery/

Artillery fire will be opened on the captured trenches without the sanction of the Guards Brigadier concerned.

(f) As regards (e) (iii):-

It is unlikely that such an attack will come as a surprise, and Commanders will have time to make suitable dispositions.

In any case, no good will be gained by reinforcing the front line.

Supporting troops must hold their ground, and by means of fire and local attacks keep the enemy in check until sufficient reserves are available to assume the offensive.

(g) All Officers must consider the action to be taken by the troops under their command in the event of attack on any portion of the front for the defence of which they are responsible. Plans must be thought out beforehand, and the action to be taken known to all. Nothing should be left to chance.

Battalions and Companies must keep each other informed of their plans to meet various eventualities.

Officers Commanding Battalions in the line will always issue a Defence Scheme to their Company Commanders. This Defence Scheme should be handed over from Battn. to Battn., on relief. It should not contain any information concerning dispositions other than those of the Battn., concerned. A copy will always be sent to Brigade H.Q.

The action to be taken by Support and Reserve Coy's. in the event of an attack should always be clearly stated, also any special tasks or special points to be defended by Lewis Guns. The action of Reserve Lewis Guns will also be laid down.

It should also be made clear that O.C., Reserve Coy's. must know the position of Units on their right and left, even though they belong to another Division or Brigade.

APPENDIX "B".

GAS ALERT.

When the wind is between N.W. and S.E. Guards Brigades in the line will send the message "ALERT" to all Units under their Command, also to supporting Artillery Group and other attached Units.

The extra precautions to be taken on receipt of this message are as follows :-

EXTRA PRECAUTIONS TO BE TAKEN DURING A GAS ATTACK.

1. All men in positions where they are liable to be suddenly overwhelmed by gas will wear their helmets rolled up and pinned on front of the coat (as per instructions G.D. 1560/G.)

2. A sentry will be posted on every tunnel dugout, or other dugout holding more than 10 men.

3. A sentry will be posted on each group of two or three small dugouts.

4. A sentry will be posted on each Hd.Qrs. and Signal Office.

5. Men sleeping in rearward lines or in works where they are allowed to take off their equipment, will sleep with their gas helmets round their necks, and must know exactly where their second helmet is to be found.

6. All gas helmets will be inspected at the commencement of every "ALERT" period in addition to the ordinary inspection.

7. R.A. sentries will be doubled.

8. An Officer on duty will be detailed from each Company in Reserve.

9. Gas helmets must always be worn outside the greatcoat.

10. Men will be forbidden to wear macintosh sheets round their shoulders, and will have the top button of their greatcoats undone.

S E C R E T.   1st Guards Bde. No. 1525.

2nd Bn. Grenadier Gds.	50th Infantry Brigade.
2nd Bn. Coldstream Gds.	119th Infantry Brigade.
3rd Bn. Coldstream Gds.	Right Group G.D.A.
1st Bn. Irish Gds.	Left Group G.D.A.
1st Guards M.G. Coy.	75th Field Coy, R.E.
1st Guards T.M. Battery.	O.C. PRIEZ Farm Battalion.
H.Q., Guards Division.	

1. Herewith 1st Guards Bde. Provisional Defence Scheme for the FREGICOURT Sector.

2. Appendices B1, B.2, C, and D are attached.

3. Appendix A is "Principles of Defence" and has been issued to all units concerned.
   More copies can be had on application to this Office.

ACKNOWLEDGE.

9th February 1917.

Captain,
Brigade Major, 1st Guards Bde.

S E C R E T.

Copy No. 15

1ST GUARDS BRIGADE DEFENCE SCHEME.

Reference Maps - COMBLES 1/10,000.
BOUCHAVESNES 1/10,000.

1. **BOUNDARIES.**

   The front allotted to Guards Division extends from U 26 c 7.5 to U 20 b 3.2. The whole of this front is held by 1st Guards Brigade.

   Southern Boundary of Divisional Area.

   U 26 c 7.5 - U 25 c 25.25 - B 6 c 7.2 - B 5 d 5.1 - B 11 c 0.6 - B 10 d 0.2 - (LE FOREST to XV Corps) - B 10 c 0.1 - B 9 d 0.0 - B 14 b 5.0 (MAUREPAS to XIVth Corps) - B 14 a 7.0 - B 14 c 3.7 - B 14 c 0.0 - B 19 a 0.4 - A 24 a 6.2 - A 24 a 0.5 - thence along North side of PERONNE ROAD to A 22 b 50.25 - across road to A 22 b 4.1 - A 22 a 7.2 - A 26 c 5.9.

   Northern Boundary Divisional Area.

   U 20 b 3.2 - U 20 a 0.7 - U 19 b 8.7 - T 30 a 8.7 - T 30 a 0.4 - T 29 b 0.2 - T 28 b 5.2 - thence along railway running through COMBLES and along valley on North side of SAVERNAKE ROAD and OAKHANGER WOODS to B 8 a 75.80 - B 7 Central - junction of roads B 7 c 4.8 - junction of roads A 12 b 9.5 - thence along Western outskirts of HARDECOURT to A 12 c 8.0 - FORKED ROADS A 18 a 05.90 - A 16 b 8.7.

   INTER-Battalion Boundary. U 26 a 4.8 - U 25 a 0.9 - U 19 d 2.2.

2. **ORGANISATION OF DEFENCE.**

   The defensive system is organised as follows :-

   A. **FRONT LINE.** - Consisting of 25 Island Posts.

   B. **SUPPORT LINE.** - Consisting of 12 Island Posts from 100 to 200 yards in rear of Front line with a strong point on either flank. (This is still incomplete). The Posts will be joined into a continuous line as soon as the ground permits.

- 2 -

C. RESERVE LINE. - Consisting of 100 yards of BLAMONT RESERVE in the Right Sector, and 200 yards of BLAMONT RESERVE in the Left Sector, connected and supported by 14 Island Posts - from 500 to 800 yards in rear of Support line.

D. INTERMEDIATE LINE.- Wired throughout and spitlocked, but not dug - from 800 to 1,200 yards in rear of the Reserve Line.

E. SECOND LINE.- Not yet traced.

3. TACTICAL FEATURES.

The most important tactical feature in the Divisional Area is the ridge which runs from RANCOURT to SAILLY-SAILLISEL.

It is just on the forward slope of this ridge that our Front Line is situated and it is of the utmost importance that the enemy should not gain possession of the ridge.

At present the enemy can only observe the high ground in neighbourhood of intermediate line from the North about LE TRANSLOY and from the S.E.

It is essential therefore to deny the enemy the observation of the FREGICOURT and LE FOREST VALLEYS, which he would gain by the capture of the RANCOURT - SAILLY SAILLISEL RIDGE.

4. DISTRIBUTION OF INFANTRY.

A. The Brigade is disposed as follows:-

Brigade Headquarters - BOIS DE DOUAGE - B.4.c.4.2.

Right Front Battalion - H.Q. - B.6.b.5.9.
    1 Coy - Front Line Posts.
    1 Coy - Support Line Posts.
    2 Coys- Reserve Line.

Left Front Battalion - H.Q. - ORCHARD - U.20.c.4.6.
    1 Coy - Front Line Posts.
    1 Coy - Support Line Posts.
    2 Coys -Reserve Line.

Brigade Reserve - 2 Battalions - Camps, MAUREPAS.

B. The Battalion of the Guards Brigade in Divisional Reserve PRIEZ FARM is also for tactical purposes under the orders of G.O.C., 1st Guards Brigade.

5. ARTILLERY.

The Brigade Front is supported by Guards Divnl. Artillery, divided into Right and Left groups. One of these Groups is told off for each Battalion Front:-

RIGHT GROUP - H.Q., ARDERLU WOOD - B.11.a.4.7.

LEFT GROUP - H.Q., T.28.a.9.6.

6. **ACTION IN THE EVENT OF ATTACK.**

   (a) The C.O. and Company Commanders of Battn's coming into reserve at PRIEZ Farm must at once reconnoitre the ground and best cross country tracks between PRIEZ Farm and the Reserve Line.

   (b) Battalions in reserve at M'UREPAS must be prepared to move on receipt of orders and C.O's and Company Commanders must reconnoitre the ground and best cross country tracks to PRIEZ Farm as soon as possible after arrival in the Camps at M'UREPAS.

   (c) The Reserve section of Bde. M.G. Coy will move without awaiting Orders to the old German gun pits at U 25 a 2.7.

   (d) The two Reserve Sections of the Trench Mortar Battery will be prepared to move as ordered.
   All Officers of the Battery will reconnoitre the Reserve Line and the best means of approach to it.

   (e) The Field Coy., will stand to in billets and await Orders.

   (f) All fatigue and other parties will report at once to the nearest H.Q.,

7. **GAS.** In the event of Gas Attack, Gas Alert or Gas Shell Bombardment, Units will act upon 4th Army Standing Orders "Defence against Gas".

8. The following plan for a counter attack on the SAILLY-RANCOURT Ridge from the Reserve line is issued as a guide to Commdg., Officers and Company Commanders in thinking out their own plans :-

   (a) There will be a heavy preparatory bombardment on that part of the line which has been lost.

   (b) Preliminary Movement: By Zero the assaulting Battalions or Companies from Brigade Reserves will have moved, under cover of darkness, to assembly positions immediately in front of (East of) and close to the wire protecting the Reserve Line.

   (c) At Zero the Creeping Barrage will remain stationary for 1 minute, 200 yards in front of Reserve Line and will then advance :-

   Zero plus 1 minute - 25 yards.
   Zero plus 2 minutes - 50 yards.

   and continue to advance at the rate of 50 yards per minute, to the line of our present "S.O.S." Barrage, where it will remain stationary.
   The stationary barrage on the line referred to in (a) above will be lifted when the creeping barrage reaches it.

(4)

(d)   Orders for the lighting of flares by the assaulting troops will be notified at the same time that the Zero hour is notified to Battalions.

(e)   A supply of flares to be kept in the Reserve Line, PRIEZ FARM, and MAUREPAS CAMPS for this purpose.

(f)   If a Contact Aeroplane appears, Flares will be lit by our troops still occupying positions in the Front and Support Lines after a successful enemy attack, in order to locate the exact area held by the enemy.
A supply of flares will be kept in the Front and Support Lines for this purpose.

-:-:-:-:-:-:-:-:-

[signature]

Captain,

9th Feb: 1917.   Brigade Major, 1st Guards Brigade.

APPENDIX "B.1".

DISPOSITION OF MACHINE GUNS.

1. **FRONT LINE SYSTEM** - 6 guns.

    H.1. Strong Point U 26 c 7.5. 1 gun firing E., S.E., & S.
    (proposed)
    H.2.   U 26 a 5.0.   "   S.E.
    H.3.   U 26 a 35.60.   "   E. & N.E.
    J.1.   U 20 c 4.3.   "   N.E.
    J.2.   U 20 b 0.2.   "   N.E. (enfilading
                                                     support line
                                                     wire).

    J.3. Strong Point U 20 a 3.5.   "   N. & N.E.
    (not yet complete).

2. **RESERVE LINE SYSTEM** - 4 guns.

    K.1.   U 25 d 0.2.   1 gun firing E. & S.E.
    K.2. K.3.   U 19 d 2.7.   2 guns firing N.E. & S.E.
    L.1.   U 19 d 3.8.   1 gun firing S.E.

3. **INTERMEDIATE LINE** - 2 guns.

    M.1.   (Proposed - no gun in position).
    M.2.   T.30 d 1.85.
    M.3.   T 30 a 9.2.

4. **BRIGADE RESERVE** - 3 guns.

    German Gun Pits - U 25 a 0.5.

    (NOTE : Guns in Strong Points on flanks of front line
    system are not yet in position, as the Strong
    Points are not yet complete. These guns and
    the third gun in Intermediate line are at
    present FREGICOURT.

APPENDIX "B.2."

DISPOSITION OF STOKES GUNS.

    1 Gun - (offensive, with dug-out)   -   U.26.a.2.1.
    1 Gun - (defensive)   - U.23.a.2.4.
    1 Gun - (defensive)   - U.20.c.4.0.
    5 Guns- Brigade Reserve.   - PRIEZ FARM.

APPENDIX "C."

MEDICAL ARRANGEMENTS.

Wounded will be carried by hand or rail to Bearer Posts at RANCOURT (C.1.a.3.2.) and PRIEZ FARM (S.8.a.3.5.) for the Right Battalion in the line, and at the FREGICOURT - SAILLISEL SAP ROAD (T.24.b.6.0.) and FREGICOURT (T.30.a.4.7.) for the Left Battalion in the line. From PRIEZ FARM and FREGICOURT Bearer Posts, wounded and sick will be evacuated by motor ambulances to A.D.S. at OO BELL (T.23.d.8.9.) and thence to TROMPT WOOD A.D.S. (C.30.a.7.3.), from which they will be evacuated to XIV Corps Main Dressing Station or Rest Station respectively by M.A.C.

APPENDIX "D".

The S.O.S. telephone message or rocket means thatb the enemy are actually leaving their trenches to attack, and that rapid barrage is required from the Artillery and from Machine Guns that can barrage our front line.

The S.O.S. signal rocket for XIV Corps is one green, one white, one green rocket fired in quick succession and repeated until acted upon by the Artillery.

Th S.O.S. signal rockets for XV Corps is a single red and white rocket repeated at intervals until acted on.

==*=*=*=*=*=*=*=*=*

334/4

SECRET.   G.T.No. 2691/1/G.

G.D.A.
C.R.E.
1st Guards Brigade.
2nd Guards Brigade.
3rd Guards Brigade.
Pioneer Battalion.
A.D.M.S.
XIV Corps.
20th Division.
40th Division.
"Q".

1. Appendices "A" (Gas Attack) and "C" (Gas Alert) attached to Guards Division Defence Scheme are cancelled.

The orders regarding

Gas Attack,

Gas Alert.

Gas Shell bombardment,

contained in Fourth Army Standing Orders on "Defence against Gas" will come into force in their place.

2. Medical arrangements in case of attack for attachment to Guards Division Defence Scheme are attached.

ACKNOWLEDGE.

C.P.Heywood.

Lieut. Colonel,
17th January 1917.   General Staff, Guards Division.

.D.No. 2691/1/.

APPENDIX "D".

MEDICAL ARRANGEMENTS FOR ATTACHMENT TO GUARDS DIVISION DEFENCE SCHEME.

No. 9 Field Ambulance will combine the duties of evacuating sick and wounded from the line, with those of attending and evacuating sick from PRIEZ FARM and MAUREPAS VALLEY Area.

Wounded will be carried by hand or rail to Bearer Posts at RANCOURT (O.1.a.8.2.) and PRIEZ FARM (B.6.a.3.3.) for the right battalion in the line, and at the FREGICOURT - SAILLISEL Road (T.24.b.6.0) and FREGICOURT (T.30.a.4.7) for the left battalion in the line. From PRIEZ FARM and FREGICOURT Bearer Posts, wounded and sick will be evacuated by motor ambulances to A.D.S. at COMBLES (T.28.d.8.9) and thence to TRONES WOOD A.D.S. (S.30.a.7.6), from which they will be evacuated to XIV Corps Main Dressing Station or Rest Station respectively by M.A.C.

From MAUREPAS VALLEY Camps sick are evacuated by horsed and motor ambulances to Headquarters of No. 9 Field Ambulance at MARICOURT (A.22.a.8.4) and thence to XIV Corps Main Dressing Station or Rest Station by M. A. C.

In the event of a heavy hostile attack the bearers of Nos 3 and 4 Field Ambulances at MEAULTE will be moved to MARICOURT immediately to reinforce the bearers of No. 9 Field Ambulance, and moved forward from MARICOURT as required.

SECRET

Copy No. 5

G.D. No. 2691/1/G.

Herewith Guards Division Defence Scheme.

Guards Division Defence Scheme (Provisional) is cancelled & should be destroyed.

ACKNOWLEDGE.

C P Heywood

Lieut-Colonel,
General Staff, Guards Divn.

14th January 1917.

```
Copy No. 1    General Staff.
        2    "Q".
        3    C.D.A.
        4    C.R.E.
        5    1st Guards Brigade.
        6    2nd Guards Brigade.
        7    3rd Guards Brigade.
        8    Pioneer Battalion.
        9    A.D.M.S.
       10    XIV Corps.
       11    20th Division.
       12    40th Division.
       13    War Diary.
```

*****o*****

G.D. No.8691/1/G.

GUARDS DIVISION DEFENCE SCHEME.

1. Boundaries.
2. Organisation of Defence.
3. Tactical Features.
4. Distribution of Infantry.
5. Artillery.
6. Principles of Defence.
7. Machine Guns.
8. Action in Case of Attack.

APPENDICES.

A. Gas Attack.
B. S.O.S. and Counter Preparation.
C. Gas Alert.

Sketch showing Defensive Line and Boundaries.

GUARDS DIVISION DEFENCE SCHEME.

1. BOUNDARIES.

The front to be held by the Division is from U.26.c.7.3 to U.20.b.3.2.

Southern Boundary of Divisional Area.

U.26.c.7.3 - U.25.c.25.25 - B.6.c.7.2 - B.5.d.5.1 - B.11.c.0.6 - B.10.d.0.2 - (LE FOREST to XV Corps) - B.10.c.0.1 B.9.d.0.0 - B.14.b.5.0 (MAUREPAS to XIV Corps) - B.14.a.7.0 - B.14.c.3.7 - B.14.c.0.0 - B.19.a.0.4 - A.24.a.6.2 - A.24.a.0.3 - thence along North side of PERONNE Road to A.22.b.50.25 - across road to A.22.b.4.1 - A.22.a.7.2 - A.26.c.6.9.

Northern Boundary of Divisional Area.

U.20.b.3.2 - U.20.a.0.7 - U.19.b.8.7 - T.30.a.8.7 - T.30.a.0.4 - T.29.b.0.2 - T.28.b.5.2 - thence along railway running through COMBLES and along valley on North side of SAVERNAKE Road and OAKHANGER woods to B.8.a.75.80 - B.7.central - junction of roads B.7.c.4.8 - junction of roads A.12.b.9.3 - thence along western outskirts of HARDECOURT to A.12.c.8.0 - forked roads A.18.a.05.90 - A.16.b.8.7.

2. ORGANISATION OF DEFENCE.

The defensive system is organised as follows:-

A. The Front Line system. This consists entirely of isolated posts in the front line with a few posts in close support on the left of the Divisional area.

B. The Reserve Line.

C. The Intermediate Line as shown on attached sketch. This line is wired throughout and spitlocked.

D. The Second Line (not marked out yet).

3. TACTICAL FEATURES.

The most important tactical feature in the Divisional area is the ridge which runs from RANCOURT to SAILLY-SAILLISEL.

It is just on the forward slope of this ridge that our front line is situated and it is of the utmost importance that the enemy should not gain possession of the ridge.

/At...

At present the enemy can only observe the high ground in the neighbourhood of the Intermediate Line from the North about LE TRANSLOY and from the Southeast.

It is essential therefore to deny the enemy the observation of the FREGICOURT and LE FOREST valleys, which he would gain by the capture of the RANCOURT - SAILLY-SAILLISEL ridge.

4. DISTRIBUTION OF INFANTRY.

(a) The front is held by one Guards Brigade disposed as follows

Brigade Headquarters	B.6.b.5.9.
2 Battalions	(In front, support and reserve lines.
2 Battalions	MAUREPAS.

(b) One Guards Brigade in Divisional Reserve.

Brigade Headquarters) 3 Battalions) Machine Gun Company) Trench Mortar Battery)	(BILLON FARM (CAMPS.
1 Battalion	PRIEZ FARM.

The Battalion at PRIEZ FARM is for tactical purposes under the orders of the G.O.C. Guards Brigade holding the line.

(c) One Guards Brigade in Corps Reserve.

Brigade Headquarters	VILLE.
2 Battalions	MEAULTE.
1 Battalion	VILLE.
1 Battalion	MERICOURT.
Machine Gun Company) Trench Mortar Battery)	TREUX.

5. ARTILLERY.

The Divisional front is supported by Guards Divisional Artillery, divided into Right and Left Groups, also by two Siege Batteries (208th Siege Battery, 6" Howitzers - and 25th Siege Battery, 8" Howitzers).

Right Group (Colonel BETHELL)	H.Q. BOIS ARDERLU B.11.a.4.7.
Left Group (Colonel BUZZARD)	H.Q. T.28.a.9.6.

6. PRINCIPLES OF DEFENCE.

The following principles will be adopted in holding the line:-

3.

(a) The front line will be held as thinly as is consistent with security. To permit of thus holding the front line, good wire entanglements are necessary, good arrangements for flank defence, and close and continuous observation on the part of Artillery F.O.Os.

(b) Troops will NOT fall back from one line to any other line, but all ground will be defended as long as possible whether the flanks are turned or not.

(c) There are three kinds of attack which may be anticipated:-
   (i) A raid.
   (ii) An attack on a minor scale to capture some locality, accompanied by a bombardment.
   (iii) A serious attack preceded by a heavy bombardment.

(d) As regards (c) (i):- Vigilance, active patrolling, combined with a good system of listening posts and wire make the failure of such attacks certain.

(e) As regards (c) (ii):- Should the enemy succeed in establishing himself in our trenches, he should be counter attacked immediately from both flanks and from the support trenches where such exist and are in sufficiently close proximity.

The extent and intensity of the enemy's preparatory bombardment, if closely observed, should give an indication of his objective and enable preparations for counter attack to be made before his attack is delivered. If the immediate counter attack is not successful a strong counter attack preceded by artillery preparation will be carried out from the Reserve Line. Artillery fire will not be opened on captured trenches without the sanction of the Guards Brigadier concerned.

The Guards Brigadier in the line will consider in detail the manner in which he would organise such an attack by night or day, and will discuss with G.O.C. Guards Divisional Artillery the manner in which the artillery preparation and subsequent barrages would be arranged. Suitable artillery O.Ps. to deal with any enemy force establishing themselves on the RANCOURT - SAILLISEL ridge should be selected and wires buried to them.

/(f).

(f) As regards (c) (iii) :- It is unlikely that such an attack will come as a surprise, and Commanders will have time to make suitable dispositions.

In any case, no good will be gained by re-inforcing the front line.

Supporting troops must hold their ground, and by means of fire and local attacks keep the enemy in check until sufficient reserves are available to assume the offensive.

(g) All Officers must consider the action to be taken by the troops under their command in the event of an attack on any portion of the front for the defence of which they are responsible. Plans must be thought out beforehand, and the action to be taken known to all. Nothing should be left to chance.

Brigades, Battalions and Companies must keep each other informed of their plans to meet various eventualities.

7. MACHINE GUNS.

(a) Machine guns of the Guards Brigade in the line will be distributed in depth, a proportion being placed in position just in rear of the front line system so that any further advance of the enemy beyond the front line system can be checked.

Not less than four machine guns will be kept in position in the Reserve Line, and not less than two machine guns in the Intermediate Line.

(b) G.O.C. Guards Brigade in the line will mention in his Defence Scheme the action, in case of attack, of any guns of his Machine Gun Company kept in reserve and not allotted to positions.

(c) In the event of attack the O.C. Machine Gun Company of the Brigade in Divisional Reserve will be prepared to push guns forward to previously reconnoitred positions in the Intermediate Line.

ACTION IN CASE OF ATTACK.

(A)　　The Brigade in Divisional Reserve will be prepared, on receipt of orders, to concentrate in the neighbourhood of PRIEZ FARM, Brigade Headquarters moving on receipt of orders to Divisional Headquarters at MAUREPAS.

It is essential that Commanding Officers and Company Commanders of the Brigade in Divisional Reserve should know the ground, and best cross country tracks, between MAUREPAS and the Intermediate Line.

(B)　　The Brigade in Corps Reserve will be prepared to move on receipt of orders.

****

APPENDIX "A".

GAS ATTACK.

In case of a "GAS ATTACK", the alarm will be spread by every available means.

Telephone operators will send "GAS" to all concerned.

Infantry, Lewis guns, and machine guns will open a steady regulated fire on the German trenches.

Artillery will open a deliberate fire on the German trenches and get ready for rapid barrage in case of receipt of "S.O.S." message, or on seeing the "S.O.S." rocket signal.

<u>NOTE</u>. In spreading the alarm for Gas Shell bombardments, Strombus horns, gongs, and other signals for a gas attack will not be employed.

****

APPENDIX "B".

S. O. S. and COUNTER PREPARATION.

1. The "S.O.S." telephone message or "S.O.S." rocket signal means that the Germans are actually leaving their trenches to attack, and that rapid barrage is required from Artillery, and from machine guns that can barrage in front of our front line.

2. Counter Preparation will be ordered by XIV Corps or the Division in case of information being received of a hostile bombardment of such nature as to indicate a probable hostile attack.

3. The tasks allotted to 4.5" Howitzers and Heavy Artillery in case of "S.O.S." or "Counter Preparation" being sent are shewn in attached table.

G.D.A./819/6/2/A.

....
....

COUNTER PREPARATION AND S. O. S.

1. Owing to certain changes in the Corps Artillery, Appendix 2 of Guards Divisional Artillery Defence Scheme is cancelled and the accompanying table will be substituted.

2. Registration on tasks will be carried out as early as possible and a report sent to this Office on completion.

3. ACKNOWLEDGE.

                                                        Major R.A.,

11th Feby, 1917.   a/Brigade Major, Guards Divnl: Arty.

Copies to:-

    R.A., XIVth Corps.
    Guards Division.
    1st Guards Brigade.
    14th Corps Heavy Arty.
    Right Group (Copy per Battery).
    Left Group (Copy per Battery).
    105th Siege Battery.
    208th Siege Battery.
    Guards D. A. C.
    17th Divnl: Arty.

Appendix 2.

COUNTER PREPARATION AND S.O.S.

Reference Map 57C S.W.4. 1/10,000.

The following will be the points to be fired on at Counter Preparation and S.O.S.

1. COUNTER PREPARATION.

RIGHT GROUP.	4.5" (How) Battery.	Trench Junction U.26.a.68.24. and trench 25 yards each side.
LEFT GROUP.	4.5" (How) Battery.	
	1 Section.	Trench Junction U.20.d.1.3.
	1 Section.	Trench Junction U.20.d.95.76. to U.21.c.00.78.

208th SIEGE BATTERY. (6-inch).

1 Section.	Trench U.20.d.14.40. - 55.60.
1 Section.	Trench Junction U.26.a.62.62. and 25 yards each side.

105th SIEGE BATTERY. (6-inch).   Trench U.9.a.25.12. to U.9.c.15.60.

2. S.O.S.

RIGHT GROUP.	4.5" (How) Battery.	Search ground for 50 yards each side of U.26.b.70.35.
LEFT GROUP.	4.5" (How) Battery.	
	1 Section.	Block ISOLDE ALLEY U.21.c.85.85.
	1 Section.	Block Trench U.21.a.76.10.

208th SIEGE BATTERY. (6-inch).

1 Section.	Block Communication Trench U.26.b.00.42.
1 Section.	Block Communication Trench U.26.b.0.6.

105th SIEGE BATTERY.(6-inch).   Communication Trenches about U.20.d.4½.0.

3. At S.O.S. 18-Pdrs: will form barrage along whole front as near to our Trenches as safety allows; as situation clears they will be concentrated on front on which the attack is being launched.

4. At S.O.S. and Counter Preparation the rate of fire for the first 10 minutes will be rapid with the exception that 18-Pdrs: will fire at the rate of 3 rounds per gun a minute.

At the conclusion of the 10 minutes rapid the rate of fire will drop to

    18-Pdrs: 3 rounds per Battery per minute.
    4.5" Hows.   2 rounds per Battery per minute.
    Heavy Arty.   1 round per Battery per minute.

This rate will continue until stopped by orders from this office.

In order to stop the fire as soon as possible all Commanders will frequently report on the situation, and whether continuance of the fire is necessary.

5. Tasks allotted by Corps to Reinforcing, Counter Battery and Long Range Gun Groups on Right Division Front are :-

(a) COUNTER PREPARATION.

Heavy Howitzer Battery.

    1 Section.   Trench Junction U.26.d.55.98 and 25 yards each side of it.

    1 Section.   Trench U.26.b.70.60. - 85.58.

60-Pdr: Battery.   Tracks running along the Northern Edge of ST.MARTINS WOOD and Sunken Road in U.21.b.

60-Pdr: Battery.

    1 Section.   Enfilade from U.26.b.7.4. - U.21.b.25.20.
    1 Section.   Enfilade from U.26.b.35.30. - U.27.b.35.10.

(b) S. O. S.

Heavy Howitzer Battery.
    1 Section.   Trench Junction U.26.b.60.02.
    1 Section.   Trench Junction U.26.b.70.62.

Heavy Howitzer Battery.

    1 Section.   Trench Junctions round U.21.b.4.1. and Sunken Road where trench Crosses it at U.21.b.5.2.
    1 Section.   U.21.b.47.98.

Tasks for 60-Pounders as for Counter Preparation.

Page 2,
APPENDIX "B".

ORDERS FOR COUNTER PREPARATION AND S.O.S.

Reference Map 57C S.W. 4, 1/10,000.

The following will be the points to be fired on at Counter Preparation and S.O.S.

1. <u>COUNTER PREPARATION.</u>

<u>RIGHT GROUP.</u>	4.5" (how) Battery.	Trench junction U.26.a.68.24 and trench 25 yards each side.
<u>LEFT GROUP.</u>	4.5" (how) Battery.	
	1 section.	Trench junction U.20.d.1.3.
	1 section.	Trench U.20.d.95.76 – U.21.c.00.78.
208th SIEGE BATTERY (6 inch)		Enfilade Trench U.26.a.62.58 – 73.76.
105th SIEGE BATTERY (6 inch)		Trench U.20.d.12.38 – 53.61.

2. <u>S.O.S.</u>

<u>RIGHT GROUP.</u>	4.5" (how) Battery.	Block BEECH LANE U.26.d.2.7.
<u>LEFT GROUP.</u>	4.5" (how) Battery.	
	1 section.	Trench junction U.20.d.1.3.
	1 section.	Trench U.20.d.95.76 – U.21.c.00.78.
208th SIEGE BATTERY (6 inch)		
	1 Section.	Block communication trench U.26.b.00.42.
	1 Section.	Block communication trench U.26.b.0.6.
105th SIEGE BATTERY (6 inch)		Communication trenches about U.20.d.4½.0.

3.   At S.O.S. 18 pdrs. will form Barrage along whole front as near to our trenches as safety allows; as situation clears they will be concentrated on front on which the attack is being launched.

4.   In Counter Preparation 18 pdrs. will fire on hostile front line trenches with H.E.

5.   At S.O.S. and Counter Preparation the rate of fire for the first 10 minutes will be rapid with the exception that 18 pdrs. will fire at the rate of 3 rounds per gun a minute.
      At the conclusion of the 10 minutes rapid the rate of fire will drop to

      18 pdrs.   3 rounds per Battery per minute.
      4.5" Hows.   2 rounds   "   "   "   "
      Heavy Arty.   1 round   "   "   "   "

This rate will continue until stopped by orders from this office.

In order to stop the fire as soon as possible all Commanders will frequently report on the situation, and whether continuance of the fire is necessary.

Page 3,
APPENDIX "B".
****

6. Tasks allotted by Corps to Reinforcing, Counter Battery, and Long Range Gun Groups on Right Division Front are:-

(a) <u>COUNTER PREPARATION.</u>

Heavy Howitzer Battery.

    1 Section   Trench junction U.26.d.55.98 and 25 yards each side of it.

    1 Section   Trench U.26.b.70.60 - 85.58.

60 pdr. Battery.   Tracks running along the Northern edge of ST. MARTINS WOOD and Sunken Road in U.21.b.

60 pdr. Battery.

    1 Section   Enfilade from U.26.b.7.4 - U.21.b.25.20.
    1 Section   Enfilade from U.26.b.35.30 - U.27.b.35.10.

(b) <u>S. O. S.</u>

Heavy Howitzer Battery.

    1 Section   Trench junction U.26.b.7.0.
    1 Section   Trench junction U.26.b.68.60.

Heavy Howitzer Battery   Trench junctions round U.21.b.4.1 and sunken road where trench crosses it at U.21.b.5.2.

Heavy Howitzer Battery.

    1 Section   Trench junction U.15.d.48.00.
    1 Section   Trench junction U.22.a.5.7.

Tasks for 60 pdr. Batteries the same as for Counter Preparation.

****

APPENDIX "C".

GAS ALERT.

When the wind is between N.W. and S.E. Guards Brigades in the line will send the message "WIND DANGEROUS" to all units under their command, also to supporting Artillery Group and other attached units

The extra precautions to be taken on receipt of this message are as follows:-

EXTRA PRECAUTIONS TO BE TAKEN DURING A GAS ALERT.

1.   All men in positions where they are liable to be suddenly overwhelmed by gas will wear their helmets rolled up and pinned on front of the shirt (as per instructions G.D. No.1566/G).

2.   A sentry will be posted on every tunnel dugout, or other dugout holding more than 10 men.

3.   A sentry will be posted on each group of two or three small dugouts

4.   A sentry will be posted on each Headquarters and Signal Office.

5.   Men sleeping in rearward lines or in works where they are allowed to take off their equipment, will sleep with their gas helmets round their necks, and must know exactly where their second helmet is to be found

6.   All gas helmets will be inspected at the commencement of every "ALERT" period in addition to the Ordinary inspection.

7.   R.A. sentries will be doubled.

8.   An Officer on duty will be detailed from each Company in Reserve

9.   Gas helmets must always be worn outside the greatcoat.

10. Men will be forbidden to wear mackintosh sheets round their shoulders, and will have the top button of their greatcoats undone.

Cancelled

*****O*****

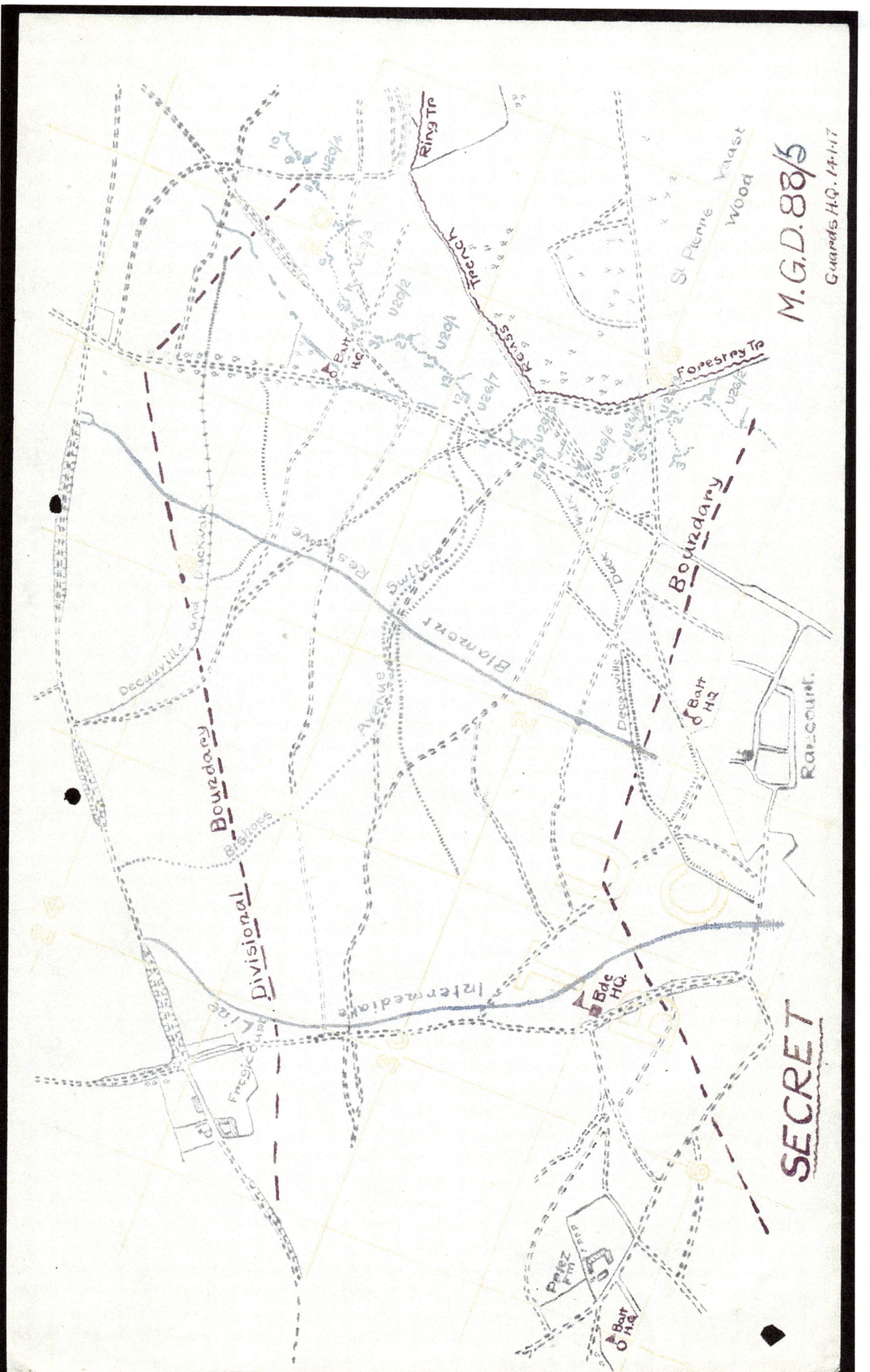

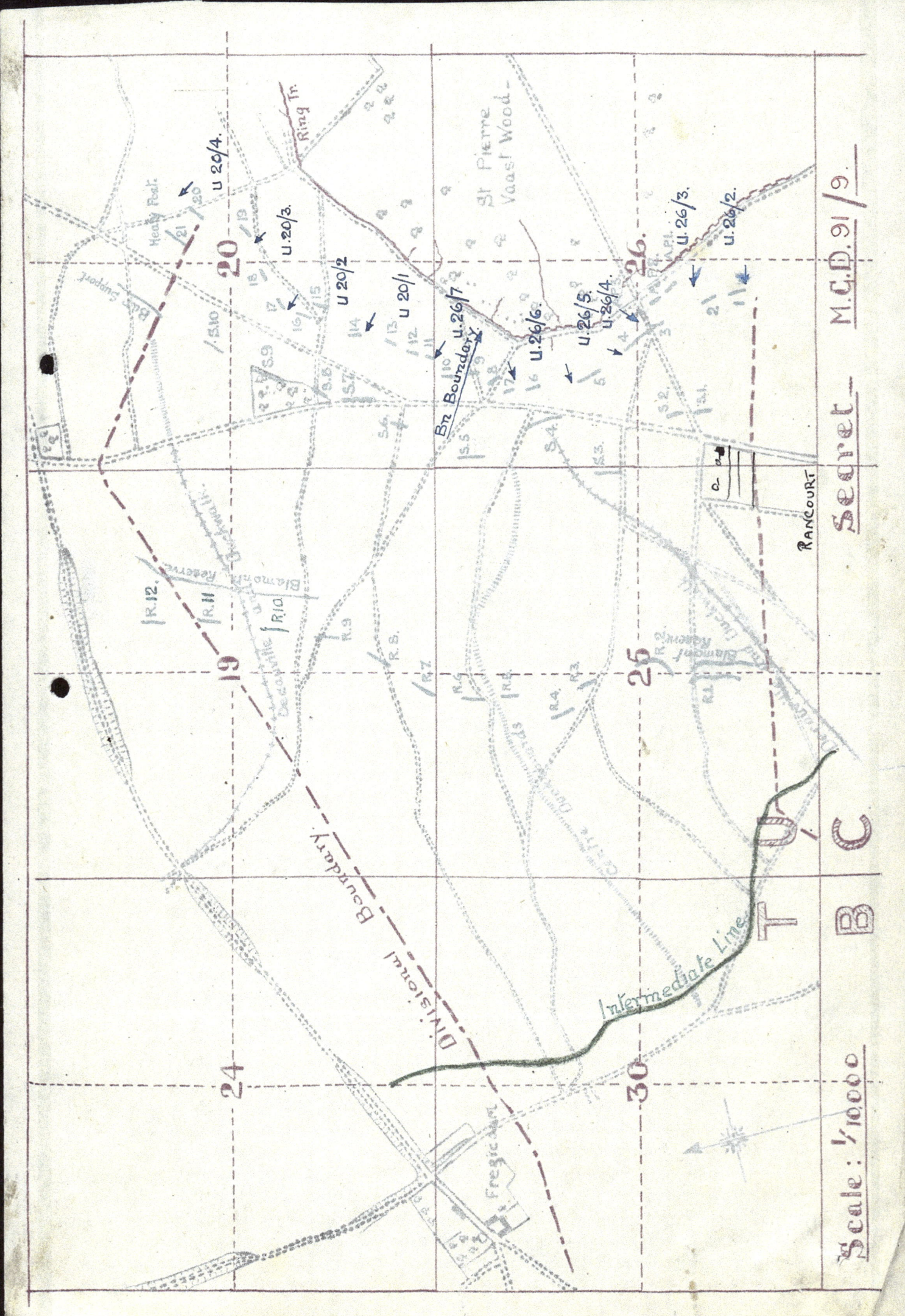

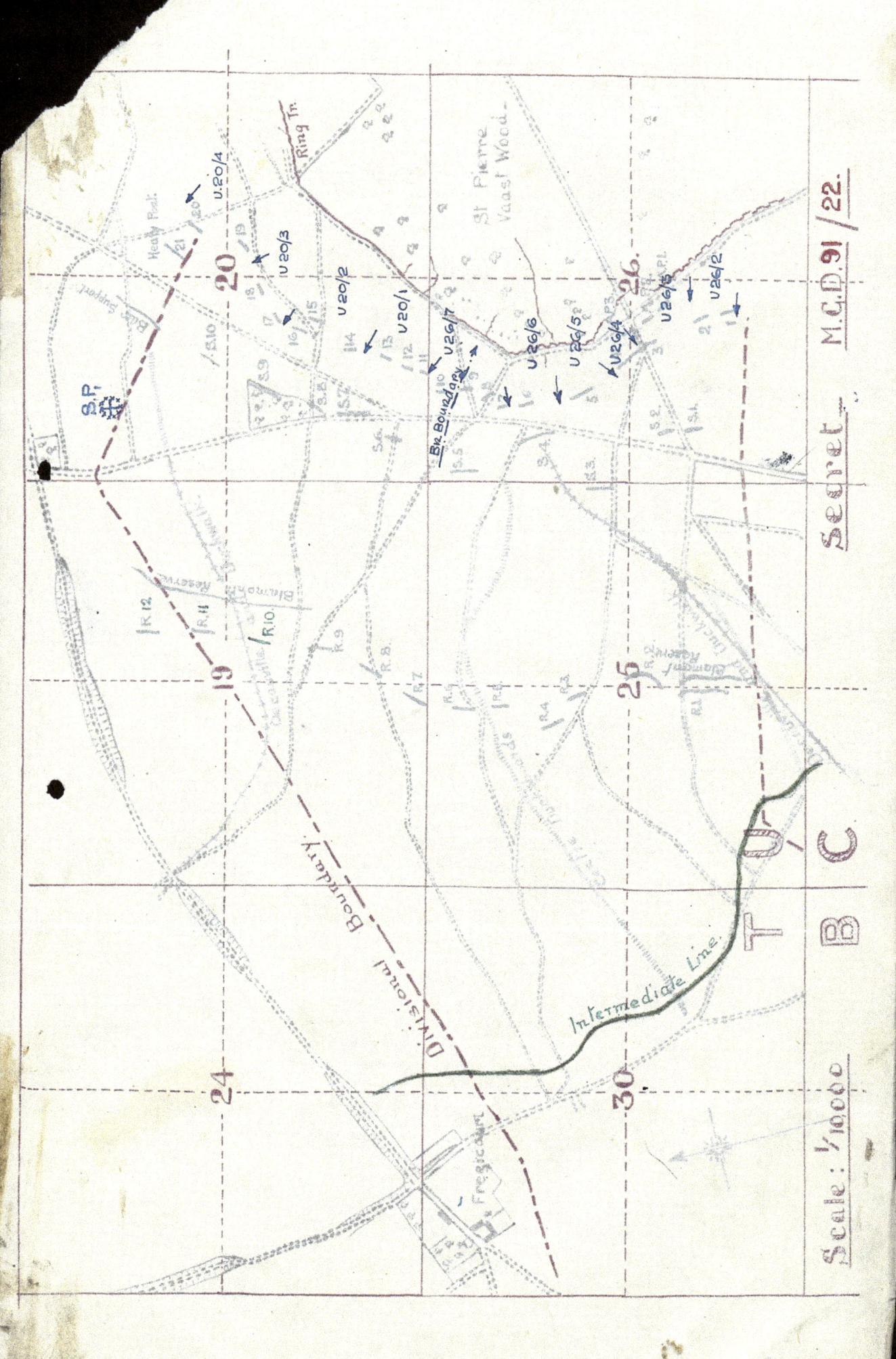

SECRET

AMENDMENT TO GUARDS DIVISION ORDER NO. 112.

Para. 7 is cancelled.

The sector to be taken over by the 3rd Guards Brigade, i.e., U.15.c.0.0 - U.8.B.2.2 will remain under the command of G.O.C. 29th Division until 10 a.m. on March 5th, at which time G.O.C. Guards Division will take over command of the new front.

<u>A C K N O W L E D G E</u> .

R O Hambro Capt
for Lieut-Colonel,
General Staff, Guards Divn.

3rd March 1917.

Issued to "Q".
         G.D.A.
         C.R.E.
         1st Guards Brigade.
         2nd Guards Brigade.
         3rd Guards Brigade.
         Pioneer Battalion.
         Divnl. Signals.
         A.D.M.S.
         A.D.V.S.
         A.P.M.
         Divnl. Train.

S.S.O.
D.A.D.O.S.
Town Major MAUREPAS.
Camp Comdt. BILLON.
Camp Comdt. BRONFAY.
Town Major MERICOURT.
Town Major VILLE.
D.G.O.
XIV Corps.
20th Division.
29th Division.
40th Division.

SECRET.   Copy No... 5

GUARDS DIVISION ORDER NO. 112.

1. The Division will extend its left, relieving portion of 29th Division, relief to be completed by 10 a.m. on March 5th.

    (a) 2nd Guards Brigade will on night of 3rd/4th March extend its left as far as U.15.c.0.0, relieving portion of 87th Inf. Bde.

    Command of this portion of the line will be taken over by G.O.C., 2nd Guards Brigade on completion of relief.

    (b) 3rd Guards Brigade will on night of 3rd/4th March relieve portion of 87th Inf. Bde. on the front U.15.c.0.0 - U.14.B.3.8.

    (c) 3rd Guards Brigade will on night of 4th/5th March relieve portion of 86th Inf. Bde. on front U.14.B.3.8 - U.8.B.2.2.

    G.O.C., 3rd Guards Brigade will take over command of Sector U.15.C.0.0 - U.8.B.2.2 at 10 a.m. on March 4th.

2. Details of reliefs will be arranged between Brigadiers concerned.

    Movements will be carried out in accordance with Appendix 'A'.

    Distribution of the Division on completion of relief is shewn in Appendix 'B'.

3. Inter-Brigade boundary on completion of relief is shewn on attached Sketch map.

    Northern Divisional boundary will be as shewn on sketch attached to G.D.No. 2709/2/G of 22nd February.

4. The Artillery supporting the Divisional front will be divided into two groups, one group supporting each Guards

/Brigade

.2.

Brigade frontage.

   Hd. Qrs. Right Group - BOIS DOUAGE.

   Hd. Qrs. Left Group - COMBLES.

5.   C.R.E. will arrange with C.R.E., 29th Division details of relief of R.E. units.

  A.D.M.S. will arrange with A.D.M.S., 29th Division details of relief of Medical units.

  Arrangements to be submitted to this office.

6.   Secret Maps, and Defence Schemes will be taken over on relief.

  List of trench stores taken over will be forwarded to this office.

7.   G.O.C., Guards Division will take over command of the new front at 10 a.m. on March 4th.

A C K N O W L E D G E.

CPHeywood.

Lieut.Colonel,

26th Feb. 1917.   General Staff, Guards Division.

Issued at 7/15 p.m.

Copy No. 1 General Staff.   14 S.S.O.
   2 "Q".   15 D.A.D.O.S.
   3 G.D.A.   16 Town Major, MAUREPAS.
   4 C.R.E.   17 Camp Comdt, BILLON.
   5 1st Guards Bde.   18 Camp Comdt, BRONFAY.
   6 2nd Guards Bde.   19 Town Major, MERICOURT.
   7 3rd Guards Bde.   20 Town Major, VILLE.
   8 Pioneer Battn.   21 D.G.O.
   9 Divnl. Signals.   22 XIV CORPS.
   10 A.D.M.S.   23 20th Division.
   11 A.D.V.S.   24 29th Division.
   12 A.P.M.   25 40th Division.
   13 Divnl. Train.   26 War Diary.

****

APPENDIX 'A'.

MOVEMENTS OF BATTALIONS ETC DURING RELIEF.

DATE	UNIT	FROM	TO	REMARKS
March 2nd	4/Grenadier Guards	VILLE	COMBLES	By rail.
	2/Coldstream Gds.	VILLE	BRONFAY CAMP,15 (2)	29th Div. will be clear of this Camp by 12 noon.
	3rd Gds.Bde. M.G. Co. and T.M.Batt.	TREUX	MAURIPAS	By rail.
March 3rd	4/Grenadier Guards	COMBLES	LINE.	
	3rd Gds.Bde. M.G. Co. & T.M.Batt.	MAUREPAS	LINE.	
	1/Welsh Guards	MERICOURT	COMBLES	By rail.
March 4th	3rd Guards Bde H.Q.	VILLE	COMBLES.	
	1/Welsh Guards	COMBLES	LINE.	
	2/Scots Guards	PRIEZ FM.	MAUREPAS.	
	2/Irish Guards	MAUREPAS	PRIEZ FM.	
	1/Grenadier Guards	MERICOURT	FREGICOURT.	By rail.

NOTES. (a). Times of trains, also detraining and entraining stations will be notified later.

(b) Battalions moving East of MEAULTE will march in file with 200 yards between Coys.

Appendix 'B'.

2ND GUARDS BRIGADE.

Headquarters	. .	BOIS DOUAGE.
2 battalions	. .	FRONT SYSTEM.
1 battalion	. .	PRIEZ FARM.
1 battalion	. .	MAUREPAS.
76th Field Coy. R.E.		

3RD GUARDS BRIGADE.

Headquarters	. .	CATACOMBS, to move later to T.17.D.6.3.
2 battalions	. .	FRONT SYSTEM.
1 battalion	. .	FREGICOURT & HAIE WOOD.
1 battalion	. .	MAUREPAS.
55th Field Coy. R.E.		

1ST GUARDS BRIGADE IN DIVISIONAL RESERVE.

Headquarters	. .	BILLON FARM.
3 battalions	. .	BILLON CAMPS.
1 battalion	. .	BRONFAY CAMP, 15 (2)
75th Field Coy. R.E.	. .	MAUREPAS.

DIVISIONAL HEADQUARTERS . . MAUREPAS.

PIONEER BATTALION will remain in present position.

****

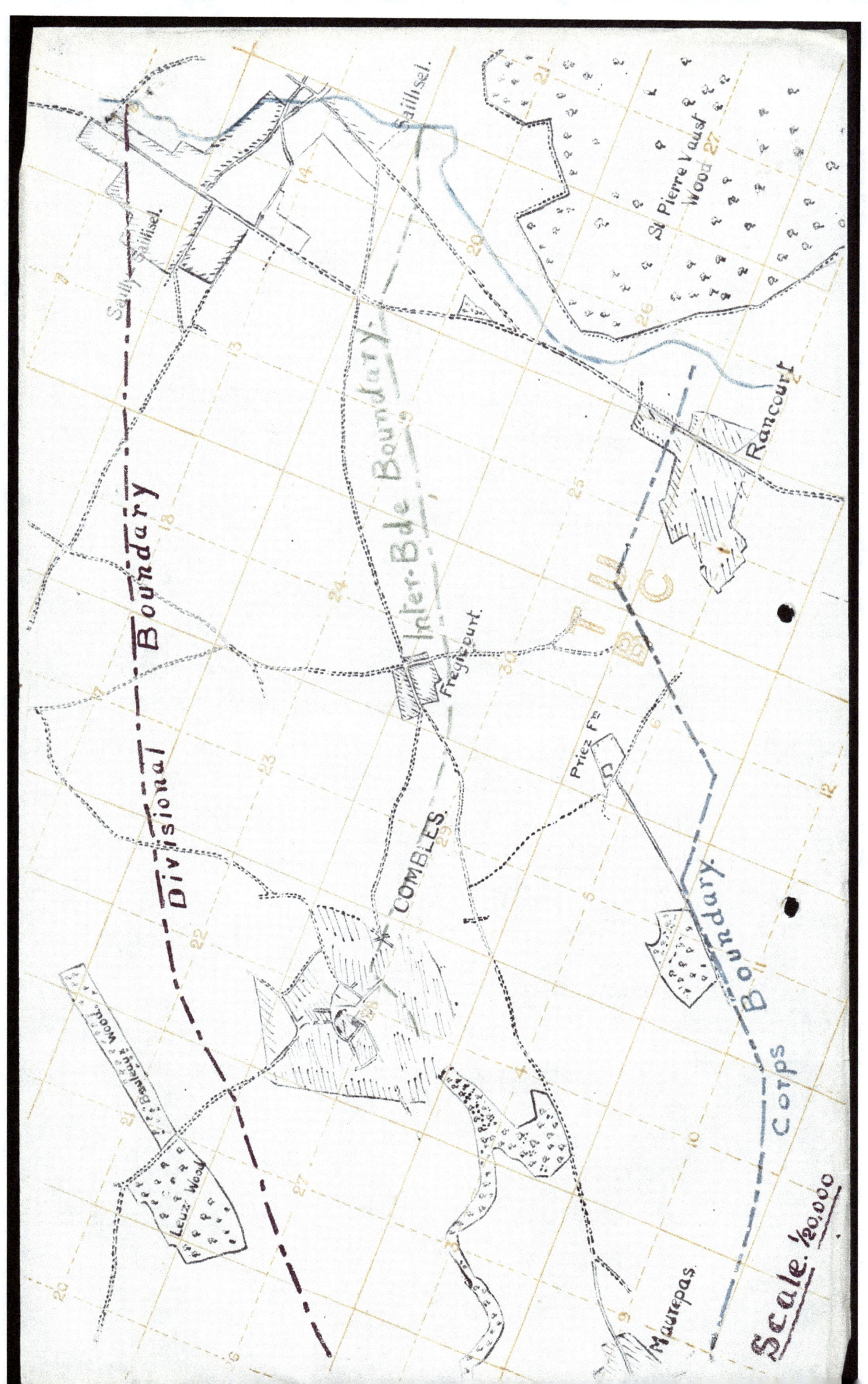

SECRET.

AMENDMENT TO GUARDS DIVISION ORDER NO. 112.

Owing to no trains being available for movements of battalions of 3rd Guards Brigade forward from VILLE and HERICOURT, Appendix 'A' of Guards Division Order No. 112 is CANCELLED, and the attached Appendix substituted.

ACKNOWLEDGE.

C.R.Heyworth

Lieut. Colonel,
General Staff, Guards Division.

27th Feb. 1917.

Issued at 11.30 p.m.

To General Staff.	S.S.O.
"Q".	D.A.D.O.S.
G.D.A.	Town Major, MAUREPAS.
C.R.E.	Camp Comdt, BILLON.
1st Guards Brigade.	Camp Comdt, BRONFAY.
2nd Guards Brigade.	Town Major, MERICOURT.
3rd Guards Brigade.	Town Major, VILLE.
Pioneer Battn.	D.G.O.
Divnl. Signals.	XIV Corps.
A.D.M.S.	20th Division.
A.D.V.S.	29th Division.
A.P.M.	40th Division.
Divnl. Train.	War Diary.

****

AMENDED COPY.   Guards Division Order No.112.

APPENDIX 'A'.
MOVEMENTS DURING RELIEF.

Date.	Unit.	From.	To.	Remarks.
Mar. 1st.	4th Grenadier Gds. 3rd Gds Bde.M.G.Coy & T.M.Baty.	VILLE.	BRONFAY. BILLON.	
Mar. 2nd.	4th Grenadier Gds. 3rd Gds Bde.M.G.Coy & T.M.Baty. 1st Welsh Guards. 2nd Coldstream Gds.	TREUX. BRONFAY. BILLON. MERICOURT. VILLE.	COMBLES. MAUREPAS. BRONFAY. BRONFAY.	
Mar. 3rd.	4th Grenadier Gds. 3rd Gds Bde.M.G.Coy & T.M.Baty. 1st Welsh Guards. 1st Grenadier Gds.	COMBLES. MAUREPAS. BRONFAY. MERICOURT.	LINE. LINE. COMBLES. BRONFAY.	
Mar. 4th.	3rd Gds Bde.Hd.Qrs. 1st Welsh Guards. 1st Grenadier Gds. 2nd Scots Guards. 2nd Irish Guards.	VILLE. COMBLES. BRONFAY. PRIEZ FARM. MAUREPAS.	COMBLES. LINE. FREGICOURT. MAUREPAS. PRIEZ FARM.	

NOTES: (A) Battalions moving from VILLE or MERICOURT will be clear of their billets by 12 noon.

(B) 29th Division are arranging to be clear of camps at BRONFAY by 12 noon on 1st and 2nd March.

(C) Battalions moving East of MEAULTE will march in file with 200 yards between Companies.

S E C R E T.

Copy No.

1st Guards Brigade Order No. 103.

Ref. Map - ALBERT 1/40,000.   February 27th, 1917.

1. (a) By 10 a.m. March 5th the Division will extend it's left as far North as U.8.b.2.2.

   (b) The front will be held by 2nd Guards Brigade on the right and 3rd Guards Brigade on the left.

   (c) The Dividing line between Sectors held by 2nd and 3rd Guards Brigades will be U.15.c.0.0.

2. The 2nd Bn. Coldstream Guards will move from VILLE to BRONFAY Camp 15 (2) on March 2nd - not to enter BRONFAY Camp 15 (2) before 12 noon.

   Route - any desired.

3. Billeting party will report to Camp Commandant BRONFAY at 9 a.m. on March 2nd.

4. 1st Line Transport will move in rear of the Battalion.

5. An interval of 200 yards will be left between Coy's. moving East of and through MEAULTE.

ACKNOWLEDGE.

Captain,
Brigade Major, 1st Guards Brigade.

Issued at 8-30 p.m.

Copy No. 1 2nd Bn. Grenadier Gds.   Copy No. 6 1st Guards T. M. Battery.
        2 2nd Bn. Coldstream Gds.   7 Guards Division.
        3 3rd Bn. Coldstream Gds.   8 1st Gds.Bde. Supply Officer.
        4 1st Bn. Irish Gds.   9 1st Gds.Bde. Transport Officer.
        5 Bde., Machine Gun Company.   10 Camp Commdt., BRONFAY.